Wounded Justice and the Story of Indian Police

James Vadackumchery

2001
Kaveri Books
New Delhi-110002

First Published in 2001
ISBN 81-7479-045-4

Published by : **Rakesh Goel**
Kaveri Books
4697/5-21 A, Ansari Road
New Delhi-110 002 (India).

Tel. : 328 8140, 324 5799
Fax : 011-719 9029
E-mail : kaveribooks@vsnl.com

Laser Typesetting by : Aarati Computers, Delhi-110 009

Printed at : Chawla Offset Printers, Delhi-110 052

PRINTED IN INDIA

To

Mary
Neethu and Neethie

Contents

Preface

Wounded Justice and the Story of Indian Police tells us the story of policing and their administration of justice down the centuries. The story begins in 1765, with the wresting of the Dewani of Bengal for the East India Company from Shah Alam II, by Robert Clive at Patna. The Company thus became the *defacto* ruler of Bengal. The Company got the control of the financial administration of three provinces — Bengal, Bihar and Orissa. The Company paid a few lakhs of rupees to the Mughal Emperor and the Nawab of Bengal and it did so from the revenue it collected from Bengal, Bihar and Orissa. The Company did not have the responsibility of policing the provinces as it was invested with the authority of Nawab. In other words, the Company received revenue without any responsibility or accountability for running the State machinery. Necessarily, such an arrangement would bring administrative anarchy and financial chaos. Doubtlessly, the Nawab could not function without sufficient finance with him or financial support. Law and order had to be maintained. But how? This task of maintaining law and order was passed on to the Zamindars and by the police forces kept by them. The Company was more keen in acquiring revenue from India and was not at all caring of policing justice administration. The Zamindari police was wholly ineffectual and inefficient. Naturally, such a police system would ensure only lawlessness and anarchy. This situation affected adversely the business interest and revenue collection of the Company. Lord Cornwallis (1786-93) the Governor General, therefore, divested the Zamindars of their police powers. He disbanded their police forces. He wanted to form a new police system and he decided to put it exclusively in the charge of the officers of the Company. Again here, the ultimate objective of the Company was not to create a people friendly police system - rather was aimed at collecting revenue by the aid and support of the police force. Whatever that be, we must admit that it was the first attempt to create a police system in India. Lord Cornwallis (vide Regulation XXII of 1793) divided the districts into police jurisdictions (each district was roughly 20 sq. miles) and he put them under darogahs. They functioned directly under the control of the European district officers. The district officers were the district collectors, or the district judges, or the district magistrates. The police stations or *thanas* thus came into existence and the darogahs received reports of the occurrence of crimes. They took the offenders into custody and produced them before the magistrates within 24 hours. The cities were divided into wards and each ward was put under a darogah. He reported to the City Kotwal who was a native officer. The City Kotwal was under the direct control of the European Collector, Judge or Magistrate. For villages, there were village watchmen who reported once a week or fortnightly at police stations. The darogahs conveyed information of serious offences committed in their jurisdiction to the neighbouring darogahs and to the magistrates of their own and neighbouring districts. Darogahs extended mutual helps for the apprehension of criminals. The strength of a police station would be one station writer, one or more jamadars, ten or more *burkandazas* (constables) armed with matchlocks. Even today, what we see is a police organization almost similar to the one established then. In other words, the police system that we have today is, in essentials, one set up by the British over two hundred years ago in Bengal. A similar system with slight modifications was established thereafter in other two presidencies and provinces in India.

How did the police then investigate cases? Did they have the expertise and knowledge to do so in a just way? How did they administer justice? How did they get police training, human formation, intellectual capabilities? Could they offer just justice?—or did they offer *wounded justice*? or did they administer justice? Perhaps, all those things were not the concerns of the Company at that time. The Company was, as stated earlier, interested only in the collection of revenue and the police was only a tool for the same. The Company wanted peace in society and for that it wanted a police system and the ultimate intention was to make money as much as possible.

The history of Indian police would show that a civil police system came into existence by the close of the 18th century. The colonial rule was certainly guided by principles which guided the Europeans in administration of justice there to some extent and doubtlessly influenced by philosophies which were in vogue in Europe. The colonial rule insisted that the suspects in a crime ought to be produced before the magistrates within 24 hours after their arrests. Before that, such a provision was not there and the reasons for enforcing such a restriction on police might be to ensure fair justice to the suspects. The same provision of law has been continuing till now and even now. Nevertheless, allegations are there that the police retain the arrestees even beyond 24 hours in police custody incommunicado. Human rights activists consider that the practice, if it exists, is not only a human right violation, but also an administration of "*wounded justice*". Hence, they ask: "why should the police have 24 hours prior to the production of the arrestees before the magistrates?" They ask further: "Why cannot the police arrest a suspect and produce him before the magistrate and get him remanded to police custody, if that is needed?" According to them, this provision of law - i.e., 24 hours detention in police custody prior to production of the arrestees before the magistrate - has been a constant source of misuse by police leading to administration of wounded justice. It is time now to study the relevance of this centuries old provision of law in the changed milieu of justice administration.

As stated above, the control of police was entrusted to the close supervision of district officers. In effect, the district officers (particularly the district collectors) found little or no time for supervising the *thanedari* police as they were busily and primarily engaged in the collection of revenue. The control of police was transferred to the district judges, but they were heavily preoccupied by their judicial functions and they got no time to supervise the *thanedari* police. When the magistrates had the control of the police, they had to face a lot of problems with the district collectors. They did not like magistrates who were junior to them in age, length of service and in administrative hierarchy to exercise control over the police which was a powerful force at that time. As far as the administration of justice by the police was concerned, one could see that there was maladministration and miscarriage of justice. The *wounded justice* resulted as a result of no effective control over the police by the district officers. Studies conducted on the police system revealed that there was corruption in police. Police was considered as an oppressive wing and there was no effective supervision over them.

As the district officers could not supervise the *thanedari* police, a suggestion was put forward and it was for favour of appointing supervisory officers within the police department. Necessarily, it meant that there ought to be police supervisors to control police stations and invariably, such a suggestion irritated the district officers who resisted the move by their tooth and nail. They thought that their authority would then be lessened and the appointment of police supervisors would adversely affect their vested interests. Hence, they shot down the suggestion on grounds of economy. What did it mean? It meant nothing but satisfaction of vested interests more than administration of justice. The history of *wounded justice* administration is probably as old as the police system in India. The police in India was quite unpopular and its extreme unpopularity with the people forced the Government to give special attention to the police system so that they could administer justice to people. This happened during 1830s. At about this time, a new police force was established in London by the enactment of the Metropolitan London Police Act of 1829. The most distinguishing feature of the said Act was the removal of the control and direction of the police from the magistrates to police commissioners. East India Company wanted to know whether or not it could apply the principles laid down in the said London Act to Indian police system. Thus the Bird Committee was appointed in 1838.

Departmental supervision of police functionaries was recognized and the Committee recommended that posts of superintendents general of police for provinces and superintendents of police for districts should be created for effective supervision of the police and for ensuring efficiency in police work. Efficiency in police force for them was more for ensuring law and order in the jurisdiction than for administering justice to people. One doubts very much whether or not the creation of superintendents was intended for eliminating the extent of *wounded justice* administered by the police in India.

In 1848, the Governor of Bombay recommended the appointment of superintendents of police in districts and thus the first district superintendents of police were appointed in Bombay in 1850. However, the London Metropolitan Police model was rejected stating that it was unsuitable for India. Certainly, it was unsuitable as the police in India was only a force for the colonial rule to plunder the Country. How could the colonial administration think of enforcing the London Metropolitan Police model in India where the British had only one interest and that was collection of revenue and nothing more. As pointed out earlier, all the district officers were Europeans and logically the district superintendents of police were put under the administrative and operational control of the district collector-cum-magistrate. Nevertheless, in 1856, the British desired to have a thorough reform of police in all provinces of India. They wanted one general plan for India modified according to circumstances. A police commission was appointed in 1860.

Indian Police After 1860

Police Commission - 1860 made many recommendations and one of the most important recommendations was that the police in each province should constitute one force under an inspector general of police whose main responsibility was to maintain it in a state of efficiency. The Police Commission - 1860 could see the police only as a FORCE and not as a SERVICE as the objective of the British was to keep the Indians under the coercive power and force of the police in India. As the police was basically and primarily a force for the British then, it went without saying that the police was not at all meant for administering justice for the people. The Police Commission 1860 recommended that there should be a superintendent of police in every district and he would be responsible for the management of the *police force* as well as maintenance of order and prevention and detection of crime subject to the general administrative control of the district magistrate whose orders he was bound to follow in all matters. These recommendations were incorporated in the Police Act of 1861.

The issues raised would be—

1. Was the police which administered justice a force? Administration of justice ought to be with fair-mindedness and not at all with the force which the police had. History revealed that the police force acted as a force during the investigation of criminal cases and when it detected criminals. Use of third degree methods, informal arrests, illegal detentions etc. could be the manifestations of the *Force Approaches* in police force. Police was never called a service and as such it could never resort to *Service Approaches* in police functionings.The *Force Approaches* were responsible for the administration of *wounded justice* in the Country.

2. Maintenance of order was an objective of the police force and certainly, the British wanted a force to maintain order in India. They gave the training to police in such a way that the police could function as a force. The British entrusted the duty of preventing and detecting crimes to this *Police Force* which could not see that administration of justice ought to be done with fair-mindedness and justness and not with the force and muscles of the police. The question would be: "could a FORCE administer justice to crime-doers in just way?"; "would not *wounded justice* be the after effect of employing force during the investigation of crime?"

3. How could a *Force* be an angel of administering justice? Certainly it could not and the history proved that it did not. Hence, now there is a growing demand for bifurcating police into two - i.e., (1) *law and order* and (2) *crime investigation*. The former may resort to Force Approaches and the latter may have recourse to Service-Approaches. In any case, a Force Approach ensures only *wounded justice*.

Though the Police Act of 1861 empowered the POLICE FORCE to prevent and detect crimes, it did not enrich the police force with adequate expertise to do the detective and preventive work. The fist - approach of the police FORCE committed atrocities everywhere and the Torture Commission - 1855 brought out the fact that the police employed force and torture.

On October 2, 1902, the Indian Police Commission was appointed and it submitted its report in May 1903. The Commission again treated the police as a Force and recommended reforms within the ambit of the Indian Police Act - 1861. The police was categorized into four - namely,

1. a *European Service* recruited entirely in England,
2. a *Provincial Service* recruited entirely in India,
3. an *Upper Subordinate* Service consisting of inspectors and sub-inspectors and
4. a *Lower Subordinate Service* consisting of head constables and constables. The post of the deputy inspectors general of police was created for ranges. Again, a new grade of deputy superintendent of police was created and police circles were made under the charge of inspectors. The officer in charge of a police station was made to be a sub-inspector and not a head constable

The Indian Police Commission: 1902-03 recommended the creation of an armed reserve in each district in charge of a European Inspector assisted by a European Sergeant. It was intended to deal with local disturbances and often it did so with iron hands. Again a provincial railway police force and a provincial C.I.D. were created and they were put under the charge of a deputy inspector general of police.

The Indian Police Commission: 1902-03 spoke about training, but nothing much about administration of justice by police. The training syllabus would show that scientific investigation of crime and psychological interrogation of suspects etc had no place. The trainees were exposed mainly to out-door training and the intellectual input was zero. The training was aimed at the development of a *parade-ground* discipline, robust physique, *yes sir - no sir* attitude, toughening the body etc. and not at all for a fair and just investigation of crimes, detection of criminals for administering just justice. *Wounded justice* was rated to be just justice by Indian police. A person living in darkness can not see the beauty of light and thus a police force which believed in the muscle strength, fist-approach, animal like behavior could not appreciate the beauty of human rights friendly approaches in justice administration. They could not make distinction between fair justice and *wounded justice.*

In London, Sir Robert Peel when he became the prime minister could introduce a Bill in the Parliament for improving the police there. As shown earlier, the Metropolitan London Police Act was passed in the summer of 1829 in England. There was stiff opposition for Sir Robert Peel, but he could see that the new police appeared in the London streets for the first time on 29 September, 1829. The whigs were not reconciled to the new police. They vowed to disband the police when they came into power. They, infact, came into power the very next year, in 1830. They could not do anything because the new police in London by that time had won over the general public by their people friendly attitudes and behavior. The colonial rule in India too saw the people friendly police in London, but the rulers closed their eyes to the realities and refused to understand the changes in London. They wanted a brutal police force and they wanted to suppress the Indian masses who raised protest against the British rule. They wanted to keep the people in awe, if not in fear of authority.

India became independent in 1947. Democracy, pluralism, secularism, social justice, development, empowerment of women, uplifting of the weaker sections etc. became the aims and objectives of the people's rule in India. Necessarily, the new outlook called for a comprehensive review and reorganization of the whole structure of justice administration and police. The people are the patrons of police in a democracy and the police have to serve the needs and expectations of the common people. Most unfortunately and dishearteningly enough, the police in India is still regulated and governed by the Police Act of 1861. A National Police Commission was appointed in 1977 and the recommendations made by the Commission have remained largely unimplemented. Now many doubt seriously whether or nor the recommendations made by the National Police Commission 1977-81are of any use for the 21st century. The recommendations have become obsolete.

A new police Act was drafted by the National Police Commission, but the said Act did not take into account seriously the human rights concepts which have been recognized and safeguarded by the Protection of Human Rights Act - 1993. The Commission was unaware of the *Equal Justice System* and as such the implementation of some of the recommendations of the Commission may lead to the administration of *wounded justice* to the people.

Politicization of police today is well known. Certainly, it has its adverse effect on the image, performance and administration of justice by police. People perceive an unholy *nexus* having developed among criminals, politicians and police. The *politicization* and *nexus* can offer nothing but *wounded justice* to people. The spoiled sons of the rich and the powerful, of the affluent and the influential, of the police politicians, of the underworld kings and unprincipled men consider themselves to be beyond the reach of law — and in many cases, they are certainly so - and indulge in criminal and antisocial activities.

What sort of justice is administered to them by the police? What sort of justice is administered by police to the victims of crime? Certainly, the police, in such situations, often are pressured to offer only *wounded justice*.

Organized crimes and crime-syndicates today acquire sinister proportions and international dimensions. *Mafia* dons, fundamentalists, narco-terrorists, criminal politicians, criminal bureaucrats, corruption gangs — all of them raise questions to the sense of police justice. Cyber crimes, cyber terrorism, insurgency etc., pose further problems for the police and the police think that they can not do justice to everybody with the help of an antiquated Police Act of 1861 and by the provisions contained in the museum piece legislations like the Indian Penal Code - 1860 and the Indian Evidence Act of 1872. A sort of Parade-ground centered police training without making any attempt to professionalize the police can yield only *wounded justice*. Today, the conviction rate is going down and the acquittal rate is going up and one sees every sub-system blaming one another for the large scale acquittals in criminal cases.

I presented a research paper on the extent of *wounded justice administration* in the XXXI All India Police Science Congress held in Jammu on 1-3 December, 1999. In my paper I said: "Acquittals of police cases are abnormally on the increase. Detection in criminal cases is deplorably low. Investigation of crime is perfunctory. Abuse of police power and authority during crime investigation is often alleged." What more does one need to establish that there exists *wounded justice* administration?

Police is a sub-system that investigates crime and detect crime-doers. Dishearteningly enough the detection rate in some States is deplorably low. According to the statistics provided by the National Crime Records, Bureau, Ministry of Home Affairs, Government of India, the detection of stolen property at the national level is around 28 per cent (in 1996) and in certain States, the detection comes down to 4.9 per cent and what a deplorable situation indeed. The recovery percentage during a decade (1986-1996) was, however, observed to be the highest at 34.7 per cent in 1986 and lowest at 14.56 per cent in 1993 at the national level.

What about the percentage of acquittals in criminal cases? During 1971, it was noticed that 38.02 per cent of the cases tried by courts ended in acquittals. During 1981, the cases acquitted went up to 47 per cent. In 1991, it further went up to 52.17 per cent and during 1996, it went further up to 62.19 per cent. Frustratingly enough, when the conviction percentage is computed on the basis of the total crimes reported, it may be shockingly seen that in some States in India, it is as low as 6-8 per cent. If the convicted cases are appealed against, then the conviction percentage may be further lowered to 2 or 3 per cent to the total crimes reported. If 97-98 per cent of the cases are just acquitted by the courts of law, then the following questions are asked -

What a colossal waste of money, manpower and material in the name of administration of justice? Is it injustice? - miscarriage of justice? - or, *wounded justice* administration?

How long must the society suffer the unaffordable luxury with zero out-put? Is the investigation of crime a police gimmick? Is not the police accountable to the society which invests nearly 10000 Crores of rupees annually on police? How to make the police more professional - more ethical - more human rights friendly and more judicious in their approaches? This alone will make the police capable of administering justice to people. The people today lose their confidence on police machinery and they devise and design their own means and methods to protect themselves and to safeguard their interest. They reluctantly approach the police to get justice.

How to make the police more transparent and accountable in their work so that they can build more confidence among the people? The police today have to ensure a wholistic justice to crime-doers, to the victims, to the society and to the justice system itself. They have to work under an *Equal Justice System* wherein there is little or no scope for administration of *wounded justice.*

Wounded Justice, World Philosophies and Police

Police must first of all internalize themselves the value of justice. The philosophers of the world - East and West - speak the same thing in different tongues. The British rulers were guided by the sublime philosophies which influenced the western thoughts when they set the rules for police and law enforcement. India too had her philosophies which guided generations and they began from the vedic periods. The British rulers in India did not either care much for the western philosophies or for the eastern philosophies. They wanted a repressive police for suppressing the Indian people for their self-interests and their interests were confined only to revenue collection and nothing more. As their objective of policing was defective, doubtlessly, their efforts failed and police abuses were plenty. The British knew their failures and the Court of Directors, in their dispatch of 24 September, 1856 made it very clear. They said: "that the police in India has lamentably failed in accomplishing the ends for which it was established is a notorious fact, that it is all but useless for the prevention, and sadly inefficient for the detection of crime, is generally admitted. Unable to check crime, it is with rare exceptions, unscrupulous as to its mode of wielding the authority with which it is armed for the functions which it fails to fulfil, and has a very general character for corruption and oppression."

Whenever the police fail in the investigation of crimes, detection of criminals, prevention of criminal activities, miscarriage of justice is resulted. People feel that the system provides only *wounded justice.* In an All India Police Science Congress organized by the Bureau of Police Research and Development, one of the directors general of police said: "If one hundred post cards are sent and out of them 90 cards reach their destination, it means that the system works". He seemed to be happy at the working of the system! Logically, he concluded that a police system which ensured some convictions in the criminal cases was to be treated as an efficient system. I failed to understand his rationale in the argument particularly when I could see 98 per cent of convictions in criminal cases in some other countries. Even there, the people could evaluate the system as one promoting administration of *wounded justice* in the 2 per cent of the cases which were acquitted. Some top level police officers in the above Congress were found to be blaming the other sub-systems namely, the prosecutors, courts and public (especially witnesses) for the large scale acquittals of criminal cases in India. Certainly, it was not a solution to the issue under discussion and blaming one another did not and could not solve the problem. The administration of *wounded justice* must be stopped and effective strategies must be implemented for the same with sincerely and earnestness. For, in justice administration, two unequals are fighting and the stronger must not take advantage of the weaker. The question we face today is not whether we want a police system which ensures just justice, but how we can get a just police system. The police must be put to the use for which the society intended it and administration of *wounded justice* is not what the society wants from the police.

How to improve the Police?

This has been a question raised by people ever since India became independent and even before. No doubt, the police has to improve its image and must show to people that the system does not work for administering *wounded justice.* The members of the police service can achieve this only through their behavior and fairness in administration of justice. No cosmetic gimmickry will do it. They have to became professional, transparent and accountable and above all must be guided by sound philosophies that must ensure fair justice to people. The police functionaries must have the desirable attitudes, steadiness, mental alertness, honesty, integrity, genuiness, and adequacy of their professed motivation and commitment to do the police job. For this, they must be informed of the objectives of police work and the philosophy that inspires their work everywhere. The chapters that follow discuss them in detail.

I am writing this preface to this book on January 1, 2001 and I hope that the philosophies discussed here will guide the police in the years to come-in the 21st century-in the third millennium. I thank my wife, Mary and daughters, Neethu and Neethie for their wholehearted support to author this title when the police in India need philosophies to lead them in future. I wish to state that the views and opinions in this book are personal and they do not reflect the views of the Union Government, State Governments, Police and Home Offices. Dr. James Vadackumchery affirms that he has the moral rights to be identified as the author of this title.

James Vadackumchery

1

Introduction

The *lex talionis* of Rome and the Mosaic Code of an *'eye for an eye and a tooth for a tooth'* were, perhaps, primitive ways of administering justice. *Maat* was the word used by Egyptians for justice (about 3000 B.C.) and the word signified to them *goodness, righteousness or truth.* For the Hebrews, *Maat* meant *wisdom.* They believed: "Great is Maat: its dispensation endureth, nor has it been overthrown since the time of its maker". Justice was an eternal value for them. Hebrews said: "They that sow the wind shall reap the whirlwind" (cf. Hosea's Proclamation) and justice meant to them an equal and opposite reaction for anything one did - or, perhaps more than an equal and opposite reaction for the one who did good or bad. Thus on sees justice is a word used by people from time antiquity. Justice in dictionary (cf. The Random House College Dictionary) today means "the quality of conforming to principles of reason, to generally accepted standards of right and wrong and to the stated terms of laws, rules, agreements etc. in matters affecting persons who could be wronged or unduly favored". Conversely enough, injustice in the same dictionary means "the quality or fact of being unjust: inequity". As the second meaning, it is seen to be the "violation of the right of others, unjust or unfair action or treatment". As a third meaning, it is found "an unjust act; wrong; unfairness". Then what is the meaning of Wounded Justice?

A wound means "an injury to an organism, usually one involving divisions of tissue or rupture of the integument or mucous membrance due to external violence or some mechanical agency rather than disease". Wound also means "an injury or hurt to feelings, sensibilities, reputation etc." Wounded justice therefore means an injury to justice–an unjust act; a wrongful act; unfairness in justice administration. It means a hurt to one's feelings, sensibilities etc. when justice is administered or said to be administered. It further means the violation of the rights of others during the law enforcement or administration of justice or during the or pretended administration of justice. Wounded justice again means -

(1) anything done against the quality of conforming to the principles of reason;

(2) anything done against the generally accepted standards of right and wrong;

(3) anything done against the stated terms of laws, rules etc.

In other words, anything done against the ancient Egyptian *Maat* which meant *goodness, righteousness or truth* may be correctly called the wounded justice.

Justice has many dimensions and the first is *individualistic* which is based on an *upright conscience* possessed by an individual. In police, the individual police officer who executes the law must possess an upright conscience if he wants to avoid an administration of wounded justice - on par with goodness, righteousness and truth. The British enacted the Code of Criminal Procedure (Act XXV of 1861) which came into force from 1 January, 1862. Section 98 of the Code stated that no police officer or other person shall offer to the person arrested any inducement, by threat or promise or otherwise, to make any disclosure and added that "no police officer or other person shall prevent the person arrested, by any caution or otherwise, from making any disclosure which he may be disposed to make of his own free will". Thus, one may see that the provisions in law made threat, inducement or promise to a person arrested to be something not permitted. Threat, promise or inducement, in such cases, did not ensure justice, but offered an administration perpetuating wounded justice. The history showed that the provision of law was sometimes violated and it brought out the fact that the individual police officers were not honest in applying the individualistic scale basing on an *upright conscience.* The powers of arrest vested in police officers by the Criminal Procedure Code - 1861 were so vast that anybody could be arrested by a police officer who did not have an upright conscience. On one pretext or another, a police officer could search any house or summon any person to a police station. Studies conducted on the working of the police then gave ample evidence to prove that the police did misuse their power and authority and thereby administered wounded justice. Police officers were poorly paid functionaries, but had very vast powers. A good many of them were illiterate people who did not know anything about police procedure. Necessarily wounded justice resulted and thus the story of wounded justice has a history of atleast more than one and half a century in India.

Justice in any country has a cultural history. If wounded justice is seen today, it means that it started long back in the culture. What is the cultural dimension of wounded justice in India? The British, though wanted to administer justice in India via police, were not keen, it seems, to do so by administration of proper justice. They wanted to administer only wounded justice to Indians. John Strachey who joined the Viceroy's Council in 1868 said: "...there is nothing offensive or disparaging to the Natives of India ...Let us give to the Natives the largest possible share in administration...But let there be no hypocrisy about our intention to keep in the hands of our people those executive posts...on which, and on our political and military power, our actual hold of the country depends. Our Governors of provinces, the chief officers of our army, our magistrates of districts and their principal executive subordinates ought to be Englishmen under all circumstances that we can now foresee". Hence, whatever the British said outwardly, they never wanted to make the police to administer fair justice. They wanted the police to behave strictly in accordance to what they were told. In Jalianwala Bagh massacre, they showed their mind and when I saw a film depicting the incident, I was shocked to witness the intensity of the British diabolism. What they did was not crude injustice - not wounded justice, but gross, devilish and barbarous atrocity on human beings. Those who preached Magna Carta and the principles contained therein - those who claimed that they were the forefathers of the human rights today - were so cruel to commit human rights violations on Indians and for which they ruthlessly made use of the illiterate Indian policemen. They made the policemen their servants and they never wanted the policemen to have any accountability to the people of India. Indian policemen were made to be the arch enemies of the people and vice versa. Thus a culture got developed in the Country and the culture continued to be the same even after India became independent. When democracy was established in India, the political parties which came into power made use of the police just like what the British did. As John Strachey said, the Indian politicians wanted their principal executives to be their own party men. Even today, the same culture prevails although, the National Police Commission wanted to abolish the culture in Indian democratic set up. The allegation today is that the political higher ups decide the transfer and postings so much so that police officers who have allegiance to a particular party in power always get favourite postings and transfers. This indeed is one reason for the administration of wounded justice in the country. During 1870s, the Duke of Argyll said: "It should never be forgotten, and there should never be any hesitation in laying down the principle, that it is one of our first duties to the people of India to guard the safety of our dominion ... the maintenance and stability of our rule must ever be kept in view as the basis of our policy, and to this end large proportions of British functionaries in the more important posts seen essential". It becomes clear from what is stated above that the British never wanted a fair justice administration - rather, they wanted to guard the safety of their dominion in India and the maintenance and stability of their rule in India. That was the only policy. Justice or no Justice – that was not an issue for them. They might resort to massacre to manipulation to maintain and stabilize their rule. The culture established by them is followed even today by every political party that comes into power in Indian democracy. Whenever a new political party come into power, it shuffles the entire police hierarchy. They place their men - adherents - in strategic positions. The politicians of the ruling party interfere in police work. Studies conducted show that such politicians tell the police: *what to do and what not to do* in certain situations. They have just one interest and that is, as stated above, nothing but to maintain their power and authority or to stabilize their rule. Just like the British functionaries performed their jobs, the *yes-men in police* of the ruling political party use, misuse or abuse their power and authority for the Government in power. Accordingly, justice, injustice, miscarriage of justice and wounded justice come to play in a democratic rule. If the politicians are unscrupulous people and if the policemen are unprincipled, then the gravity and intensity of wounded justice administration may be very severe. This is what is today known as the "unholy relationship between the police and politicians". If paper reports are true, then the ruling political party misuses and abuses the police to its advantage and to the disadvantage of the opposition political parties.

Together with the cultural development of wounded justice, it is necessary to look into the social dimension of the wounded justice administration. Today, allegations are heard of *politicization* of criminals by vested interests. Newspapers write editorials on the *politicization* of criminals and of police. Police are blamed for registration of false cases against the political opponents of the ruling political party in power. Deliberations are going on in the Parliament/State Legislatures on the issue of politicizing the police. Politicizing the police means administration of wounded justice.

Wounded justice takes place in the society owing to two reasons. They are (1) the pressures of the situation and (2) the weakness of the police system, i.e., the administrative set up. The administrative set up becomes weak because it is composed of by the *yes-men* of the ruling party in Government. An individual police officer has to fight against the pressures of the situation and the weakness of the police system. This is not possible if the higher echelons in police are the *yes-men* of the ruling political parties. As for example, a sub-inspector who has a strong ego fights with the administrative hierarchy to administer fair justice, then he may be transferred and the entire matter will be entrusted to another sub-inspector who is an *yes-man*. There are instances in which the resisting sub-inspectors are told to do something in a particular manner and if they still resist, then they are at once transferred out even by wireless messages. A superintendent of police who got a wireless transfer to the Computer Center said that he was transferred out because he refused to obey the instruction from the higher level to administer wounded justice to a *Mafia* criminal who had strong connections with the ruling political parties. The impact of wounded justice administration in society is that police loses its credibility and public trust on the system. Earlier, police officers in India believed that the police was the coercive weapon of the Government in power. They believed so because they had the misconceptions of the duties and responsibilities of police. *Government police* is a concept brought by the British, but today the people say that the old *Government police* is substituted by *people's police in* a democracy.

Wounds can be of different categories such as *the incised, the lacerated* etc. Accordingly, the wounded justice in society can *be incised, lacerated* etc. After an action by the police, sometimes, commissions of inquiry are instituted and such commissions go in detail to the issue. They inquire into the police action and bring out the nature of justice, injustice, miscarriage of justice or wounded justice. The report of any commission of inquiry may be criticized as anything can not and does not satisfy the entire people in any society and particularly so in a democratic society. Therefore, social scientists may say that anything that satisfies majority of people can be taken as a good measure to decide the nature of the action. Administration of justice means administration of justice with understanding of the laws, but the police in India from its formation were not educated. In one study, it has been noted in the report (1874 -75) pertaining to police that "excluding the Bombay Town police, 28 per cent of the force only could read and write". How could the illiterate police administer fair justice? That was not of any concern to the British. They wanted a brutal police and through them they administered brutal justice in the way they wanted. Ananndswarup Gupta in his study writes: "There were complaints of the tendency of the police to make hasty arrests and to be harsh and rough in bearing... Only 897 men could read and write and nearly half of the forces was wholly uneducated. There were also several well founded charges of extortion or bribery". He continues: "unnecessary arrests were attributed chiefly to ignorance and it was stated that improvement could be looked for only as the police became better educated". The situation continued till recently until the Governments prescribed educational qualification of the policemen and still further increased their educational qualifications to be a pass in matriculation. How could such an illiterate, semi-literate or uneducated police functionaries administer proper or fair justice to people? Perhaps, the British never wanted to administer proper justice, rather they wanted to put crimes and criminals under control for their smooth rule. As stated above, there were unnecessary arrests then and if the arrests were unnecessary, then the actions following the arrests too would be unnecessary. If this was the position during 1870-80 in India, the position remained to be the same when National Police Commission studied the nature of arrests (1977-81) after a century. The Commission wrote that 60 per cent of the arrests in India were either unnecessary or unjustifiable. How could the police claim to ensure justice and satisfy the people - at least majority of them - saying that the police would not administer *wounded justice*? In other words, wounded justice administration has a long history in India and the allegation is that it continues to be so even in the 21st century.

Any police action must satisfy not only the police officer who executes it, but also the society, law, law courts and the people. In other words, it must ensure social welfare. This means that proper justice administration has an individual dimension as well as a social dimension. It has a legal dimension and a people's dimension. It must have a dimension and a dimension that transcends time and space. Whatever the police have done in the past - whatever some individual policemen have done in the past - travels a long way even after their retirement or death. Why? The reason is that wounded justice never dies. People wounded by police-justice administration never forget it. Society never tolerates it and the stigma continues. What the police in India did during the British Raj or during the internal emergency in free India are not forgotten by the people even today. People have formed associations to fight for their rights to get composition for the suffering they underwent from the police during the internal emergency period. They complain that they were subjected to wounded justice administration and torture by the police.

Police and torture go always together and torture by police is brought always to show wounded justice administration. The torture too has a long history extending to the Torture Commission-1855 or even much beyond. It continues even today. The National Human Rights Commission takes up such cases and awards compensation to the victims of police torture/atrocities committed on them. Just yesterday, I found a police officer very gloomy. I asked him; "Why?" He answered that he had the information that the National Human Rights Commission had awarded Rs. 1 lakh as an interim relief for a victim of his action/torture/misuse of authority or whatever. I cited yesterday's situation just to say that the disease which has its roots in the past continues to spread even today. In such a situation, wounded justice administration may be seen in the years to come.

Wounded Justice Hereafter

The Protection of Human Rights Act-1993 has come into force and continues to show its relevance in all areas including police administration. Looking to the past history of administration of wounded justice in British India, we had to give shape to administer proper justice to the future at the time we got independence. Pandit Jawaharlal Nehru talking in the Constituent Assembly at the midnight on 14-15 August, 1947 said: "Long years ago we made a tryst with destiny, and now the time comes when we shall redeem our pledge, not wholly or in full measure, but very substantially". Now we have celebrated the 50th anniversary of our independence and the golden jubilee of Indian Republic. Did the new turn of events in 1947 and 1950 help us to eradicate the administration of wounded justice initiated, promoted and propagated by the

British? Has our pledge to the people of India that justice would be ensured been fulfilled-if not "wholly", but "substantially"?

An extract from the report of the National Human Rights Commission for 1996-97 may answer the question. The report says: "The Commission remained deeply engaged in efforts to bring to an end the egregious violations of human rights that result in custodial death, rape and torture. Custodial violence is a calculated assault on human dignity". And whenever human dignity is wounded, to quote the Supreme Court in its judgement of 18 December 1996 in the case of D.K. Basu Vs. the State of West Bengal, the civilization takes a step backward. The flag of humanity on each occasion must fly half-mast. The Commission continues: "During the year 1995-96, 136 deaths were reported in police custody and 308 in jail custody. In the year 1996-97, however, the figures reported to the Commission were 188 deaths in police custody and 700 deaths in judicial custody...It will be observed that there has been a doubling in the deaths reported to the Commission in police and jail custody". I have no data in my hand to show the death in police custody and in judicial custody during the British past. At the same time, I notice in the debate held on *flogging* as a punishment to Indians, Sir Mordaunt Wells arguing against the imposition of such a cruel and barbarous punishment to Indians. He said that the imposition of flogging is "inconsistent with the spirit of modern legislation and inapplicable to a civilized country". The Chairman of the debate then observed: "in many parts of India, large bodies of natives regarded imprisonment as tantamount to the punishment of death and that to such person flogging was a most merciful punishment". The debates clearly showed that death in jail custody was of no special significance to the British rulers. They therefore wanted flogging for Indians. Sir Bartle Frere said: "flogging was a very useful punishment, particularly in several parts of the country where the people were in a state of semi-barbarism." He also considered flogging a *merciful punishment* and referred to it as an "absolute necessity in the case of uncivilized persons". Of course, the decision on the issue was postponed. It was most unfortunate to note that the British advocates of flogging failed to see the truth of penal history that the flogging in the west usually resulted in the death of the flogged. They could see only the semi-barbarism of the Indians and the mercy shown to such *below human beings* in India. Their admission of death in penal custody was an open confession that the conditions which prevailed in Indian jails were so inhuman that even human imagination could not conceive of. They had the Magna Carta with them and their human approach to offenders. But such philosophies had no application to Indians even when they claimed administration of fair criminal justice. Their approach was brutality and not justice as they defined in their dictionaries.

Has the situation changed now? A few cases reported by the National Human Rights Commission in their 1996-97 report may answer the question better.

(i) Deaths in alleged Fake Encounters with Police in Andhra Pradesh

These cases arose out of complaints made by the Andhra Pradesh Civil Liberties Committee (APCLC), a non-governmental organization, which alleged that the Andhra Pradesh police had staged 'fake encounters' in order to eliminate members of the People's War Group (PWG), their supporters and sympathizers. The APCLC, in their complaint, gave particulars of such encounters which they described as fake, and stated that, instead of following the due process of law in respect of the PWG, the police was restoring to "executive elimination". In some cases, the deceased were found to be only remotely connected with the People's War Group and in some others the deceased were not involved in any naxalite activity nor had they been arrested or even mentioned in any police record.

The claim of the police in each of the cases that the persons killed had committed several offences and were accused in criminal cases. Warrants for arrest, it was said, were issued against them and they were evading arrest and that the police had the right to use force for effecting arrest which could extend up to causing of death of the accused if they were involved in offences punishable with death or with imprisonment for life. The police also claimed that the deceased were the aggressors and would have killed the police-personnel had the police not fired at them in exercise of their right of self-defence. They thus sought to justify their killing on the ground that the deceased themselves were guilty of attempts to commit the murder of police personnel.

The Commission noted that the evidence on record did not show in any of the cases that any prior attempt was made by the police to arrest the deceased persons. In none of these encounters, did police personnel receive any injury while one or more persons from the other side had died. The Commission further observed that the criminal law clearly prescribed that a person who claimed the right of private defence as a cover against prosecution had to establish the same.

Entries were made in the respective police stations to the effect that the deceased made attempts to kill the police and were, therefore, guilty of the offence of attempt to murder under Section 307 of Indian Penal Code. On that basis, they were described as accused and FIRs were drawn up accordingly. The cases were, however, closed without investigation on the ground that had abated on account of the death of the accused persons. No attempt whatsoever was made to ascertain as to who were the police officers that fired the bullets that caused the respective deaths and as to whether their killing was justified in law. Attention was confined to the conduct of the deceased and not to that of the police who had caused the deaths. No attempt was made to investigate that circumstances under which the police opened fire causing death of several persons. As this appeared to be the pattern of the procedure followed by the police, the Commission felt it necessary to conclude that the procedure followed by them was opposed to law. The Commission had to indicate the correct procedure to be followed in such cases.

The police do not possess unchartered right to kill any person with impunity. They can, like any other citizen, exercise the right of private defence. When a policeman causes death in exercise of such a right of private defence it would not be an offence as provided in Sec. 96 of the IPC. That apart, Sec. 46(3) of the Code of Criminal Procedure empowers the police officer making an arrest of a person who is accused of an offence punishable with death or imprisonment for life to use of such force as may be necessary to effect the arrest which may extend up to the causing of death of such person. The police has to act within these limitations when it has to deal with situations of an encounter. When a person is killed by the bullet of a police officer in an alleged encounter it results in an unnatural death. When information about it is received by the Officer-in-charge of the police station, he has to find out if there is reason to suspect the commission of a cognizable offence. In a situation when death occurs in an encounter by the bullet of a police officer it cannot be said whether the causing of death was justified as an act done in proper exercise of the right of private defence or falling within the limits prescribed in regard to causing of arrest falling u/s 46(3) of the Code Criminal Procedure without ascertainment of facts after due investigation. The police cannot make a presumption without investigation that the causing of the death by the bullet of the police is not an offence. The correct procedure to be followed in situations of such 'encounters' is that the police officer-in-charge of the police station on receipt of information that death was caused by the firing of the police party should record that information and draw the inference that there is reason to suspect the commission of a cognizable offence. After making necessary entries, steps should be taken to investigate the facts and circumstances leading to the death admittedly caused by the bullets of the police to find out whether it was justified either in the exercise of the right of private defence or in the legitimate exercise of the power of arrest the circumstances specified in Section 46 (3) of the Cr.PC. As the police party of the same police station is involved in the firing resulting in the killing, such cases should invariably be made over to an independent investigating agency.

The Commission recommended to the Government of Andhra Pradesh to takes steps to investigate the facts and circumstances leading to the death of members of People's War Group (PWG) in alleged encounters with the police and to complete the investigations within 4 months. If the investigations resulted in the need for prosecution, steps be taken for speedy trial. In pursuance of the Commission's recommendations, the Andhra Pradesh Government have entrusted the State CID with the responsibility of undertaking detailed investigations into the death of five persons killed in the alleged "fake encounters" and the officers concerned have been instructed to complete the task within three months.

(ii) Complaints from Shri Sanjay Singh Umesh of Daltonganj, Bihar regarding police encounter killings

The complainant alleged that on 15 April, 1996, six naxalites were killed by the police at Murumdag village, Daltonganj, Bihar. The PUCL, Palamau which had earlier enquired into the matter stated that an armed group came to the village to settle a dispute. On receipt of information, the police came and encircled the members of the armed group who surrendered to the police. Thereafter, the members of the group were made to stand at different places and fired at by the police. In all, six persons were killed as a result of the firing by the police. The PUCL found that the allegation of the police that the naxalite group had attacked the police party with bombs and firearms and that the police returned fire in self-defence resulting in the death of six persons to be untrue. The armed group came in plain clothes but after their post mortem they were dressed in khaki uniforms which had neither any holes nor bullet marks on them. The dead bodies were thrown away but when there was protest by the people, six bodies were transported in a police van and cremated by the police.

On notice being issued, SP Palamau submitted his report. The report stated that the persons killed belonged to a prescribed organization, Jan Mukti Morcha, which had been committing atrocities including murder, looting etc. It further stated that the villagers had not invited these people for the settlement of any dispute. Contraband rifles were recovered from the six 'deceased extremists'. There was exchange of fire between the police and the naxalites for about two hours. The police party was attacked by the naxalites with bombs and, therefore, the police had to return the fire, resulting in the killings. All the other allegations in the complaint were denied. It further stated that the complainant was liable to be prosecuted under section 182/211 IPC for making false allegations against the police.

The Commission in its orders noted that it had occasion to examine the correct procedure to be followed by the police in cases where deaths occur in an encounter between the police and others in a batch of cases from Andhra Pradesh. That order of the Commission had been accepted and given effect to by the Government of Andhra Pradesh. The procedure followed in this case was found to be clearly inconsistent with the correct procedure explained by the Commission in the said order.

As indicated in the order of the Commission in the Andhra Pradesh case, the police officer in charge of the police station on receipt of information about the death of six persons in this case, ought to have registered cases of unnatural deaths of six persons as a result of the firing by the police party and taken immediate steps to investigate the facts and circumstances to find out as to whether the killings were justified either in the exercise of the right of private defence or in the exercise of the power of arrest under the circumstance specified in Section 46 of the Cr.P.C. As the police attached to the same police station were involved in the firing resulting in the killing, the Commission recommended that the case should be made over to an independent investigation agency namely the State CID and to complete the investigation within four months. If the investigation called for launching of prosecution, steps for speedy trial be taken. The Commission expressed the hope that compensation would be awarded by the State if the case ended in conviction.

(iii) Killings of 11 persons by Gaya police in April, 1994 in Bihar

Suo-motu cognizance was taken by the Commission on perusal of an article regarding the killing of 11 persons by Gaya Police in April, 1994 that appeared in "The Statesman" dated 19 May 1994. The People's Union for Civil Liberties, Bihar also investigated the matter and furnished its report. The findings in the report were that this was a case of cold-blooded murder of 11 persons by the police and that the story of an 'encounter' was concocted to cover up their crime and to lend a facade of legal justification to an otherwise cold-blooded murder committed on 12 April 1994, S / Shri Syed Shahabuddin, former Member of Parliament and Arjun Kumar, an advocate also sent separate complaints.

The Commission issued notice to the Chief Secretary and DGP of Bihar. In response, a report was received from the Assistant Inspector General of Police, Bihar. It was stated in the report that Case No. 62/94 was registered on a complaint about this incident from the Sub-divisional Police Officer, Sherghati in PS Mohanpur. The case was registered against the 11 deceased extremists and 100-125 other terrorists u/s 147/148/149/307/323/353 IPC 17 CLA Act, 25(B) (A), 26/27/35 Arms and 3/5 V.P. Act. On investigation, SP Gaya stated that the 11 deceased persons and other unknown persons had gathered in Masaudha forest with a view to committing offences. Two months earlier, 3 innocent persons had been killed in broad daylight and a truck and a motorcycle burnt by the extremists. It was also contended that the extremists, out of enmity, had planned to kill the MLA and also to attack the police party. It was further stated that members of the MCC (Maoist Communist Centre) had planned to commit offences on the date of the encounter. The police having come to know about it, arrived there. The 11 persons who were hiding were asked to surrender to the police. Instead of surrendering they opened fire at the police whereupon the police fired at the hiding miscreants. After several rounds of firing from both sides there was a lull. When the police went inside they found the dead bodies of the 11 persons and some firearms and explosives. A sum of Rs. 8798 in addition to arms and ammunition and some literature in which a call was given to the farmers to fight against feudalism were recovered. The others had fled away. The villagers were called to get the bodies of the 11 persons identified but nobody recognized them. After a confidential inquiry it was found that 6 out of the 11 persons who were killed were involved in Mohanpur PS Case No. 19/94 for murder of 3 persons and the burning of a truck and motorcycle and for other offences under the IPC.

On examination of the report, the Commission felt that unless the matter was inquired into by a senior judicial officer, the explanation of the police could not be accepted. With the permission of the High Court, the Chief Judicial Magistrate, Gaya has accordingly been entrusted with the inquiry.

(iv) Custodial death of Shri Bundoo in Uttar Pradesh

The Senior Superintendent of Police, Moradabad vide his fax message dated 14 October, 1995 reported the death of one Bundoo while in custody. The Commission took cognizance and called for a report from the Government of Uttar Pradesh. In their report, the Government stated that on 12 October, 1995 a case under section 302/301 IPC in crime No. 273/95 was registered at Police Station, Chandpur, Bijnore District against four named persons. The case came to be investigated by an SHO. Two of the accused persons were arrested in the morning of 13 October and on interrogation one of them described the place of incident. After being handcuffed, he was taken to the site for identification in course of investigation. He had also indicated that he would lead the police to the discovery of weapons used for the offence.

Two police SHOs along with a host of constable proceeded to the place. Suddenly, Bundoo jumped out of the vehicle and came to fall in front of a moving bus. He received serious injuries which ultimately led to his death at Moradabad District Hospital. The SSP indicated that the two Inspectors concerned had been ordered to be present at the roll call and orders for departmental action would soon be initiated

The long reports and the connected material were scrutinized by the Commission. Accepting the same to be true version of the incident, the Commission held that the deceased sustained grievous injuries when he jumped from a moving jeep and fell before a speeding bus. There was no dispute that a host of constables were also travelling in the jeep along with the deceased who had already been handcuffed. It was the obligation of the constables to ensure that the handcuffed accused would not run away from the jeep. The fact that so many police officers were present in the jeep when the deceased jumped out of the vehicle showed gross negligence by the police guard.

The Commission recommended that an inquiry be undertaken immediately and the concerned police officers and the constables, if found guilty of negligence, be adequately punished.

The Commission took the view that compensation should be paid to the next of the kin of the deceased and recommended a compensation of Rs. One Lakh in this respect. Government would be free to reimburse itself, as it considered appropriate from the delinquent police officers. It would be open to apportion the amount of recovery.

(v) Custodial death of Shri Atal Bihari Mishra, student of Banaras Hindu University, U.P.

The Commission initially received a report from the Superintendent of Police, Balia District, Uttar Pradesh, on the custodial death of Atal Bihari Mishra on the basis of which it issued notice to the Chief Secretary, UP calling for a report. The Commission also received a joint petition from Shri Shreesh Chander Dixit, Member of Parliament and Dr. Vina Pande, Member of UP Legislative Council on this case. The matter was raised in Parliament by the former Prime Minister Shri Chandrashekar who urged the Government to refer this case to the Commission.

The Commission directed a team from its own investigating staff to conduct a preliminary enquiry. Upon being informed by the State Government that the State CID was entrusted with the enquiry into the case, the Commission asked it to expedite the investigation.

On perusal of the CID report which was received by the Commission, it observed that this was an instance of police high-handedness as its worst. A young boy, because of political differences between his father and a local politician belonging to the ruling party, was dragged to the police station on "fictitious and frivolous" charges and was mercilessly roughed up. The Commission felt that unless appropriate punishment was meted out to officers responsible for this kind of crime, it would be difficult to contain and control custodial torture. The Commission, therefore, tool up this matter with the then Governor of UP urging him to ensure that charge-sheets against the errant personnel are filed expeditiously before the Court. Later, the Commission followed this up with another letter expressing serious concern over the delay and urging immediate submission of charge-sheets and departmental action against the delinquent police officers.

As a result, nineteen police officers/officials have been charge-sheeted under various sections of law in the Court of the Chief Judicial Magistrate, Balia for the Custodial death of Shri Atal Bihari Mishra, a student of the Banaras Hindu University.

(vi) Death in police custody of Shri Udayan in Kerala

The case was brought to the notice of the Commission by Dr. Xavier Paul who alleged that Udayan died in police custody in the lockup in Mannarghat Police Station on 20 January 1994. Amnesty International also reported this incident in a publication brought out by it in March 1994.

On the basis of evidence of Shri Rashid, an inmate of the same lockup, the Commission noted that Udayan was beaten up a couple of hours before his suicide in the Sub Inspector's room as also when he was being brought back to his cell. The Commission was of the view that the torture to which Udayan was subjected by the police in the lockup contributed to his committing suicide. The Commission recommended that:

(1) A case should be registered against the police officials responsible for torturing Udayan and that they should be prosecuted with utmost expedition.

(2) Payment of compensation of at least Rs.1,00,000 to the family of Udayan.

Accordingly compensation of Rs. 1,00,000/- has been paid to the family of Udayan. The Home Department, Government of Kerala has asked the Director General of Police, Kerala to register a case against the police officers responsible for torturing Udayan.

(vii) Custodial death of Shri Babulal Dhaniwal, Alias Bablu Rai in Assam

On 20 June, 1995 the officer in charge of Bihaguir Outpost under Sonipur District alongwith some other police personnel took into custody one Bablu Rai Alias Dhaniwal along with six others while they had assembled in the house of one Jagannath to attend a dinner. They brought all the seven persons to the outpost. The police personnel reportedly tortured Bablu Rai and others to extort a confession regarding a theft of a fan and thereafter put all the persons in a police lockup. The following morning, at about 04.00 A.M, Bablu Rai was found dead in the police lockup. The magisterial inquiry confirmed the fact that Bablu Rai had died in the lockup due to physical torture by the police personnel. The post-mortem report showed no external injury and the cause of death was not ascertainable as indicated therein. In the report of Deputy Secretary, Political (A) Department dated 12 September, 1995 it was stated that departmental proceedings had been drawn up against police personnel and they had been suspended.

On Commission's intervention, the State furnished the report of the magisterial enquiry where the magistrate has observed that he had come to the conclusion that Bablu was arrested alongwith other boys on 20.06.1995, brought to the Bihaguri police outpost. Severely tortured and beaten by two police officers and that he died on 21.6.1995 in the police lockup. The Commission went by the magisterial enquiry report and recommended immediate prosecution of the police personnel involved in murder.

The Commission recommended that a sum of Rs. 50,000 be paid by way of compensation to the parents of Bablu or if there be other dependents then to them. This payment be taken as interim in nature and would not preclude a claim for compensation to be laid in the appropriate forum.

(viii) Custodial death of Shri Tirath Singh in Punjab

This proceeding was initiated on information received from the Senior Superintendent of Police, Ferozpur, Punjab about the death of one Tirath Singh Jija. The District Magistrate also reported the matter vide his letter dated 15 January, 1996. According to the report the deceased was produced before the Judicial Magistrate on 1 January, 1996 having been arrested in a case under the Excise Act. The Magistrate remanded him to judicial custody for 15 days and he was taken to the Central Jail, Ferozpur. After he had crossed gate no. 1, before he was actually admitted into the jail, it was stated that he slipped due to an epileptic attack and the jail authorities refused to accept him in judicial custody. The police got him admitted into the Civil Hospital, Ferozpur for treatment and later shifted him to Baghi Hospital, Ferozpur where he died on 8 January, 1996.

The Commission was surprised to find that the Judicial Magistrate was not informed about what had happened, particularly when his direction remanding to judicial custody was not carried out. If that had been done, an immediate inquiry would have been undertaken and a clearer picture of the situation would have been available.

There was no material to support the plea that the deceased was subject to epileptic fits. The post-mortem related the cause of death to grievous injuries on the head, spleen and other vital parts of the body. The investigation did not show that these injuries were caused by the fall as a result of the alleged epileptic attack. In the absence of clear material, the

Commission was not in a position to accept the plea of the police that death occurred on account of the fall as a result of a sudden epileptic attack. The police had to account for the loss of life as the deceased was in their custody.

As ante-mortem report showed that grievous injuries were found on the body and the police are not able to account for them, the Commission inferred that those injuries were caused by torture when the deceased was in police custody resulting in his death. The Commission directed that an interim compensation of Rs. 50,000 be paid for the loss of life to the next of kin of the deceased.

(ix) Complaint from Shri P.S. Bhatia regarding alleged death of Shri Mohd. Mansoor in police custody at Baliya P.S., Bihar

The National Minorities Commission forwarded a complaint under a covering letter dated 5 April, 1994 alleging the death of Mohd. Mansoor in police custody at Baliya police station in district Begusarai of Bihar State of 5 February 1994. On issue of notice, the Government of Bihar vide their letter dated 15 September 1994, reported to the Commission that one Saiyyad Mohd Kasim was robbed of Rs. 33,105 which he was carrying while he was travelling on a bicycle. The money was meant for salaries of some school teachers and his own. Three men stopped him at pistol point and threw him on the ground from the bicycle and took away the money. On a written complaint from Shri Kasim, a case under section 392 IPC was registered and investigation undertaken. In the course of investigation the house of Mohd Mansoor was searched by the police but he escaped by the back-door. The villagers gathered there on hearing the noise, and caught hold of Mohd. Mansoor. He was taken to the police station. He was later sent to the hospital in an injured condition and given first aid. As the condition of Mohd Mansoor was serious he was advised to be sent to the Begusarai hospital where better facilities were available. The deceased is said to have died as a result of the blows he received at the hands of the public.

The matter was inquired into by the IGP, Bhagalpur and Divisional Commissioner, Bhagalpur. From the report submitted by them, there did not appear to be any cogent evidence of assault by the members of the public. On the other hand three witnesses spoke of a police assault. Seven more witneses stated that they saw the beating administered by the police. The mother and the widow of the deceased also spoke about a police beating.

The Commission felt that if the fatal injuries had really been received from members of the public, the police should have immediately taken Mohd Mansoor to the hospital instead of keeping him for a long period at the Police Station and only thereafter taking him for treatment. The Commission therefore did not agree with the findings of the investigation that the deceased met his end on account of injuries sustained by him as a result of assault by members of the public. There appeared to be an attempt by the police to shield its own officers at the lower level. The circumstances indicated that he was tortured at the police station and died as a result of the injuries he received.

The Commission called upon the Director General of Police, Bihar to ascertain within one month the names and particulars of the police officers who had taken the deceased into custody and had occasion to handle him at the police station and to prosecute them. It further recommended that an interim compensation of Rs. one lakh be paid to the widow of the deceased. The State Government was asked to consider the propriety of taking steps for recovery of the amount from the concerned delinquent police officers.

The Government of Bihar in its letter dated 28 February, 1997 intimated that a sum of Rs. one lakh has been sanctioned to the widow of the deceased. The Commission is following up on other aspects of this matter.

(x) Attempt at rape by jail official in Uttar Pradesh

The complainant alleged that a jail official in Agra had occupied her house and prostitution was practiced in its premises. On notice being issued, I.G. (Prisons) sent a report of Superintendent of District Jail, Agra wherein the allegation was accepted and the official was found guilty. It was further stated that the official has attempted to rape the wife of a Constable in premises of the jail in 1993 and, as a result, she had committed suicide. The Commission ordered on 8 August, 1996 that jail official be prosecuted.

(xi) Police torture of Shri Ram Charan Meena, A villager in Rajasthan

The Superintendent of Police, Angul, acting as complainant, stated that on 14/15 October, 1993, two police officials and a few constables led by an Additional Superintendent of Police forcibly entered into the house of Shri Ram Charan Meena of Hurla village, misbehaved, kicked and abused him and then took him away to the police station and detained him at Mahua PS. He was subsequently shifted to Manpur PS and subjected to further humiliation. A sum of Rs. 6000 was also snatched by the police from him.

On notice issued by the Commission to Director General of Police, Rajasthan, the SP (Vigilance), Rajasthan, stated that, on 15 January, 1993 the police had gone to village Hurla in search of Shri Bal Ram Meena involved in Manpur police case u/s 302, 392 IPC. The allegations that the police forcibly entered his house and snatched away Rs. 6000 was denied.

The Commission, on perusal was not satisfied with the report. Accordingly, it made an order on 10 May 1996 directing its Director General (Investigation) to ascertain the facts and report to the Commission. Accordingly, the matter was inquired into by the investigation wing of the Commission and a detailed report in this behalf filed. The findings were as follows:

(1) Shir Ram Charan Meena was assaulted by police constables.

(2) He was brought to the Police Station, Mahua and produced before SP Dausa on 15 October 1993 to find clues about an absconding person. On the way, he was also taken to Mahua about 5 kms. away from the village towards Manpur.

(3) After he was produced before SP Dausa, he was duly questioned and thereafter released in the evening.

(4) The injuries on his person were simple in nature. There was no independent evidence that they were caused by the beating by a police sub-inspector. However, the injuries were obviously caused by beating by some police constables.

The Commission accepted the findings of its investigation wing and recommended initiation of appropriate action against the offending Inspector. In regard to the role of the S.P. Dausa, the Commission was of the view that he be cautioned. The Commission directed the DGP, Rajasthan that expeditious action as recommended be taken and reported to the Commission.

(xii) Alleged Misbehavior and torture of Shri Ram Singh, A member of Cuddalore Bar Association at the hands of the police, Tamil Nadu

On receipt of a complaint from Cuddalore Bar Association alleging misbehavior and torture of Shri Ram Singh by certain police officials on 12 March, 1994 at about 10.00 P.M. the Commission issued notice to the State Government of Tamil Nadu and called for a report.

The Chief Secretary, in his report dated 21 April, 1994 stated that police personnel were obstructed on their way to a rural area on the plea that they had gone there without informing the local people and Ram Singh in particular. It was further indicated that the Sub-Inspector and Head Constable had received injuries on being assaulted by Ram Singh's group. Another report dated 27 October, 1994 was received from the Chief Secretary informing the Commission that an inquiry into the matter was got conducted through the Assistant Collector and pursuant to his report the Government of Tamil Nadu ordered the Director General of Police, Tamil Nadu to initiate severe departmental action against an Inspector of Nellikuppam Police Station. It was also reported that the Director General of Police had been directed to initiate departmental action against the Head Constable and the other police constables who participated in the activities at the police station and near Ram Singh's house.

On consideration of the matter, the Commission held that Ram Singh had been manhandled. While expressing its hope that the State Government would take serious view of the lapses of the concerned police officials and they would be adequately dealt with, the Commission recommended to the State Government to pay a compensation of Rs.5,000 to Shri Ram Singh either out of the consolidated fund of the State Government or to recover the same from the erring police Sub-Inspector.

The State Government having failed to comply with the recommendation of the Commission regarding payment of compensation, the Commission has approached the High Court of Madras for appropriate directions to the State Government in terms of its recommendations. The case is pending before the High court.

(xiii) Mass cremation of unidentified dead bodies by Punjab police: Referral by Supreme Court

Writ Petitions (Criminal No. 47/95), Committee for Information and Initiative on Punjab vs State of Punjab and others and Writ Petition (Criminal) No. 497/95, Paramjit Kaur vs Punjab and others filed before the Supreme Court of India were referred to NHRC, with the following Orders dated 12 December 1996:

"Two issues were raised before this Court in Mrs. Paramjit Kaur vs State of Punjab and others, in Writ Petition (Crl.) No. 497/95 and the connected Writ Petition (Crl.) No. 447/95. The first issue concern the abduction of Mr. J.S. Khalra, General Secretary, Human Rights Wing of Shiromani Akali Dal. This Court after monitoring has passed final order so far as issue regarding Mr. Khalra is concerned. This second issue raised in the Writ Petition related to the Press Note dated January 16, 1995 issued by the Human Rights Wing of the Shiromani Akali Dal under the signatures of Khalra and J.S. Dhillon under the caption "DISAPPEARED CREMATION GROUNDS". The Press Note stated that large number of persons were cremated by labeling them as unidentified. This Court dealt with the second issue as under:

"The second issue highlighted in this petition is equally important. This Court cannot close its eyes to the contents of the Press Note dated January 16, 1995 stated to be investigated by Khalra and Dhillon. In case it is found that the facts stated in the Press Note are correct - ever partially–it would be a gory-tale of Human rights violations. It is horrifying to visualize that dead bodies of large number of persons - allegedly thousands could be cremated by the police unceremoniously with a label "unidentified". Our faith in democracy and rule of law assures us that nothing of the type can ever happen in this Country but the allegations in the Press-Note, horrendous as they are, need thorough investigation. We, therefore, direct the Director, Central Bureau of Investigation to appoint a high powered team to investigate into the facts contained in the Press Note dated

January 16, 1995. We direct all the concerned authorities of the State of Punjab including the Director General of Police, Punjab to render all assistance to the CBI in the investigation. All the authorities of the Punjab Government shall render all help and assistance to the CBI team as and when asked by any member of the said team. We give liberty to the CBI to seek any further directions from this Court from time to time as may be necessary during the investigation".

"The CBI has completed its inquiry as directed by us. The 5th and final report was filed in this Court on December 9, 1996. The report is self explanatory and speaks for itself. The Registry shall send a copy of the report to the National Human Rights Commission (the Commission) under a sealed cover. The report indicates that 585 dead bodies were fully identified, 274 partially identified and 1238 unidentified. Needless to say that the report discloses flagrant violation of human rights on a mass scale. Without going into the matter any further, we leave the whole matter to be dealt with by the Commission.

This Court on December 11, 1996 passed the following order:

"Pursuant to this Court's order dated November 15, 1995, the CBI has placed on record the 5th and Final report dated December 9, 1996 regarding the cremation by Punjab. Mr. M.L. Sharma, Joint Director, CBI is personally present in Court. We agree with the suggestion of Mr. Sharma that the contents of the report be kept secret, as at present, because further investigation has to be undertaken by the CBI. Mr. Sharma has suggested that since large number of cases may have to be registered, the CBI may be permitted to undertake investigation of 10-15 cases and the remaining cases be investigated by the Punjab Police. We appreciate the suggestion but since the CBI has done the initial investigation in this matter and has placed five detailed reports before this Court and while appreciating the work of the CBI, we are of the view that as at present, the

CBI should undertake the investigation of all the cases which are to be registered as a result of the final report. We, therefore, direct the CBI to take further action into the matter and register the cases, where necessary hold investigations and proceed in accordance with law on the basis of the material collected during investigation.

We, however, give liberty to the CBI to seek further directions, if necessary, from this Court in line with the suggestion made by Mr. Sharma or for any other purpose. The CBI shall, after every three months, place a status report regarding the investigation in this Court".

While the CBI is investigating the matter, we are of the view that the remaining issues involved in this case be left for the determination of the Commission, which is the appropriate body for this purpose.

Learned counsel in the two Writ petitions have vehemently contended that all the 585 bodies which have been identified, their heirs/dependents are entitled to compensation. Our attention has been invited to various provisions specially Sections 12 and 18 of the Protection of Human Rights Act, 1993.

We request the Commission through its Chairman "to have the matter examined in accordance with law and determine all the issues which are raised before the Commission by the learned counsel for the parties". Copies of the order dated November 15, 1995 and all subsequent orders passed by this Court along with the Copies of all the CBI reports in sealed covers be sent to the Commission by the Registry.

Since the matter is going to be examined by the Commission at the request of this Court, any compensation awarded by the Commission shall be binding and payable. If any approval or further assistance from this Court is necessary, the same may be sought by the Commission. The necessary papers be sent to the Commission within one week in a separate seal cover".

Having regard to the magnitude and the possible ramifications of the matter and the complexities of issues of fact and law that might arise, the Commission held the view that, in the first instance, it might have to address itself to the question of evolving and formulating a procedure appropriate to the nature of the subject matter. The Commission also found it expedient to have the benefit of the views of all concerned and for that purpose it directed notices to as many as 10 parties and 4 advocates who were representing the parties in one or the other case. The matter was then further heard by the Commission on the jurisdiction, scope and ambit of the powers of the Commission under the dispensation of the Supreme Court's mandate as well as the specific issues arising for determination.

What do these illustrative cases show? They show how do the police and jail authorities administer justice in India - in free India - on her jubilee year of independence. Where does the matter go wrong?

Police Reforms for 21st Century

Government of India has now appointed a Committee on Police Reforms. The Committee has prepared a questionnaire to study the police system and functionings for making recommendations. The questionnaire contains a few questions relating to administration of fair justice. Some questions are -

(1) How can we give Indian Police an image of a cultured, people friendly police force without sacrificing the effectiveness of police?

(2) How do you think the existing gap between the public expectations and police performance can be bridged?

(3) Police handling of weaker sections and women have been coming under constant flack from all quarters. What steps can be taken to improve police behavior to the weaker sections and women?

(4) Today, police do not enjoy public trust and co-operation to the extent similar organizations do in developed countries. How do we remedy this?

(5) Do you think the present system of training is suitable for a community friendly, service oriented law enforcement agency? If not, what is wrong?

(6) Do you think the present police set up at the station level inspires confidence in the public, especially the socially disadvantaged sections? What suggestions do you have to improve the situation?

(7) It is said that 60 per cent of the arrests made by police in the Country are really unnecessary. This is in addition to the totally unauthorized detentions in the police stations which are not even recorded. An unnecessary arrest becomes the starting point for further human rights violations, like beating up in lockup etc. What steps do you think need to be taken to eliminate unnecessary arrests?

(8) Another major reason for people feeling harassed by the police is the non-registration of crime when people approach the police stations. What suggestions you have to see that the malady is rectified ?

(9) One of the constant criticisms is that the Government of the day uses the police for enhancing its political clout. The Government uses the power of transfer and postings to exercise its influence to further its end. What are your views for providing a reasonable tenure to the three important levels in police, namely the SHOs, the SSP., and DGs of police? What machinery would you suggest

to see that the transfers made are in public interest and not in political interest? What mechanisms are necessary to ensure that the police perform their legitimate duties without the fear of uncalled for interference from outside, at the same time, ensuring the accountability of the police for their acts of commissions and omissions?

(10) Political interference in police working is being depicted as a major handicap in the efficient functioning of police. Do you feel this is correct? How prevalent is it in your State?

(11) How do we insulate police at various levels from undue political interference without taking away its accountability?

There were severe criticisms in a section of the press against the questionnaire. Admitting that the questionnaire has not been prepared with a total vision of police system in a holistic way, it can not be denied that the questions put therein expose the nature, extent and intensity of wounded justice in Indian police administration. Of course the questionnaire is not exhaustive to bring to light all areas of wounded justice administration. We have some information about the British administration of justice and we have more information about the administration of justice now. The question which needs an answer is : "Is the administration of justice today better than the same in the British past?" It has to be better and no doubt the people expect a better system for the years to come.

Note

1. Anandswarup Gupta, *The Police in British India* - 1861-1947, Concept Publishing Company, New Delhi, 1979.

2

Wounded Justice and Police Under the British

'Wounded Justice'- many did not remotely think thus during the British rule in India. The Government in London saw their version of justice being administered in their colony and therefore they wanted to import a legal system to their taste in Indian territory. Thus, they brought the Indian Penal Code. Indian Police Act, Code of Criminal Procedure, Evidence Act etc. to administer a sort of criminal justice in the sub-continent. I do see now many things which are one hundred years old. Buildings which are one hundred years old become buildings of tourist attraction. Urbanization, industrialization, development of science and technology have changed the face of the world. Philosophies which ruled the world about a century ago exist no more in the world. Police philosophy of the pre-independent India is now no more than a history. Nevertheless, the penal laws, Evidence Act, Police Act etc. which are almost one and half a century old still rule the justice system in India. Necessarily, the result is administration of wounded justice in the country.

Once a pig killed a man in the west. A case was registered against the pig and the pig was sentenced to death. Though this happened in the past, people today laugh at it and say incredible. All evils die with the dead - this is an accepted principle and the dead man is not tried for awarding any punishment. The dead can not defend him before a court of law and any legal system can not accept the trial of a dead man. A dead man has no place in the array of the accused in a charge-sheet and if a dead man's name appears in a charge-sheet, future generations will say incredible. Does it happen in India now? If the answer is *yes* to the above question, then what type of justice is it? - will it not be miscarriage of justice? - be injustice proper? - be *wounded justice* ? If juvenile delinquents are treated just like or along with adult offenders, then what type of justice will it be?

Suppose, the police torture a suspect and obtain a confession from him. Later, he is convicted by a court of law. In the current understanding of the justice system, the offender is administered justice. The question is: "what type of justice" and the answer is: *wounded justice*. Why? Torture is an injury caused to an organism - it is an injury to the feelings of the suspect - and it is not a quality of conforming to the principles of reason.

Justice system is an organism and an *organism means a form of life composed of mutually dependent parts that maintain various vital processes*. It also means "*any organized body or system conceived of as analogous to a living being* and thus comes the governmental organism. Criminal justice organism, as it is today, consists of many mutually dependent parts - sub-systems - and the police is one among them, a sub-system that investigates crimes and detects criminals. The police have to abide by and execute laws strictly in accordance to accepted standards of right and wrong and to the stated terms of law, rules, agreements etc. No law, Indian and international, permits police to have recourse to arbitrary arrests. If a police officer sees that an offender is punished after a trial and he manages to get it by an arbitrary arrest of the accused, then the justice thus administered is called wounded justice. What is the relevance and meaning of incommunicado detention in police custody? It is a hurt to human sensibilities for justice administration. And how can the police claim that they assist the courts of law to administer justice when they resort to strategies that may, at best, ensure only wounded justice?

An external violence or some mechanical agency causing a division of tissue or rupture of the integument or mucous membrane is called a wound. In justice administration too, the police are blamed or accused of becoming susceptible to external pressures and political influences and forces can be many or various. Police becomes thus a means to execute the desires or the pressures which rupture the people's confidence on the system. The ruptured justice is otherwise called wounded justice. Conduct a search and humiliate a person and later say: "excuse me" and then claim that everything is done for the cause of justice administration! What is it? It is doubtlessly wounded justice, for, justice has many dimensions and above all, it must be just and fair ensuring equal justice to all concerned in the process. After a raid in a house, a mother and her only daughter committed suicide as they could not bear the social humiliation and disgrace caused to them. They were not there on the earth to hear the verdict from the court of law declaring that they were totally innocent.

A criminal-centered justice system and that was how the Code of Criminal Procedure-1861 thought about justice administration in the 19th century. A crimino-centric system can offer only *wounded justice*. A criminal is not everything - or - all in justice administration. A criminal does not live in an island - in vacuum. When the justice system administers criminal justice to the crimedoers alone, the system administers injustice, wounded justice or miscarriage of justice to many others in society - and to the justice system itself. Police, for example, registers a false case against a fellow citizen, then it offers disservice to the system itself. The system is not intended to do such nefarious activities and if it does so, it paves the way to administer injustice proper which is highly sinister in character.

An Agency for Social Control

An agency for social control and to control human behavior has been in existence in some form or other from the beginning of man. For, man can not live without he being controlled by internal, external and in many cases by both forces.

"When we men, O Varuna, commit an offence before the heavenly host, when we break the law through thoughtlessness, have mercy on us. Almighty, have mercy on us"-Rg.Veda (1,25). People were afraid of God and they thought that man committed crime because of demenological influence and his innate deprivity. They prayed for the mercy of God and in the west, they resorted to exorcism to get themselves free from devil's influences and consequent commission of crimes. Could exorcism evict devils from man? In any case, exorcism could cause severe pain to the one believed to have been possessed by the devil. A devil centered administration of justice was in every sense an injustice, but no one in the past thought in that way.

In the Old Testament, God himself was the detector of crime and administrator of justice. When Adam and Eve violated the divine commandments by eating the fruits of the forbidden tree, the Yahweh God asked the woman: "what is this you have done?" In Genesis (Gene; 3:8) one reads: "The woman replied, the serpent tempted me and I ate". After detection, the Yahweh God punished the serpent, the woman and the man.

The Buddha said: "confess before the world the sins you have committed" and sins implied violation of the rules, laws or regulations. The Buddha prescribed the *Eightfold Path* of self - development which led to the State of Buddhahood and in such a state, no policing was necessary. "Right knowing, right seeing, dealing with right action, right meditation etc.", the Buddha said, "could take people to the final goal" - i.e., *Nirvana* which is equivalent of moksha in Hinduism. There was no necessity for an external agency to control man and his behavior if he was prepared to become good by removing the false notions of a separate self from himself. Was it possible for every human being to become so? Certainly not and therefore it became necessary to have some agency for social control and man's behavior. In due course of time, the agency thus created was known as police and the work it did was called policing. The agency was to ensure justice to people and justice is a concept that undergoes changes. "All things arise and pass away" - said the Buddha and perhaps the concept that the flow and change were the basic features of nature could be noticed at the root of Buddhism. The concept of justice, police justice, police sense of justice could also undergo changes during the passage of time. What was considered as justice once could be treated as injustice, wounded justice, miscarriage of justice at another time. The concepts are in a state of constant evolution and it goes without saying that what the British thought as justice for Indians in 1860 when the Indian Penal Code was drafted could be wounded justice today. For example, a person who commits cheating of another person for a small amount and a professional cheat who manages a crime-syndicate are treated alike by police in the presently existing penal laws. I could see a case in which a misappropriator of property worth Rs. 3 crores and another of property worth Rs. 600 were treated alike and more honestly, the former misappropriator was a privileged one before the police as he was affluent and otherwise influential with the police. Discrimination of people on the basis of influence/affluence is certainly unjust and to that extent leads to administration of wounded justice.

Police of the British India, the Independent, India and Wounded Justice

Did the British establish a police system in India for administration of just justice? - total and full justice? - equal justice? I do not think that the British wanted that. They wanted to strengthen their rule and for that they desired prompt suppression of all challenges to their rule. They wanted a police system to do the job and their intention, it was found, was to develop a sense of fear among the Indians so that they did not threaten the British to continue their rule, exploitation and realization of maximum revenue from the Country. The British appointed a Police Commission in August 1860 and the Commission was told to keep in mind that the "*functions of a police are either protective and repressive or detective*". 'Repressive' did not mean administration of just justice and the word 'protective' did not have any significance in the background of what the police did under their 'repressive' force or power. On the basis of the draft Bill prepared by the Commission, the Police Act (V of 1861) was enforced in India. The Act could keep the people of India effectively repressed by the police force thus created. Punitive police, repressive police, threatening police which came into being, doubtlessly, could administer only wounded justice to the people under their control in India.

Nineteenth century witnessed the reign of *utilitarianism* in England. *Utilitarianism* maintained that the greatest good of the greatest number of people ought to be the philosophy of life. The nineteenth century utilitarian philosophers in England did a lot of things - lectures, writings, publishing journals and establishing a political party etc. - for improving the economic and political conditions of their country. For, people in England were the people for them. In order to protect the interest of their people in England and in India, they wanted to supress the people of India and to repress their emotions against an alien rule. Police became thus a necessity and thus came an organized police force in India. The philosophy which guided the British was utilitarianism which they described as *altruistic hedonism*.

Jeremy Bentham (1748-1832) and John Stuart Mill (1806-1873) were the ablest exponents of utilitarianism in England. Police force in India was considered by the British as a 'utility' for them and nothing more. If they were to administer criminal justice in India, it was understood only in terms of the *utility* involved. Bentham said that it was not the motives, but the consequences of what one did that counted in everything and the consequences of what the police did in India were to establish the British rule here. A good policing ought to promote the greatest happiness of the greatest number of people, and not the interests of the privileged few. But, the police during the British raj promoted only the interests of the privileged few - i.e., the British people - precisely therefore, they could administer only *wounded justice* to the people in India. For example, the Code of Criminal Procedure -1861 empowered the police to arrest practically any person and detain him in custody for atleast 24 hours. They could, on one pretext or another, search any house at any time and could call any person to a police station just by writing an order for the purpose. Could such provisions of law ensure fair justice? History had proved that they could not and today, the courts insist the issue of *custody memo/arrest memo* etc. and to show due respect to human rights and human dignity. Administration of wounded justice to Indians and utilitarian benefits to the English - this was behind the enactment of the Police Act, Code of Criminal Procedure etc.

John Stuart Mill was employed by the East India Company. Mill maintained the view that the utilitarian standards of conduct, "when rightly understood must be not the agent's own greatest happiness, but the greatest amount of happiness altogether". When the British enacted the Police Act - 1861 for repressing the Indians, they bought about their pleasure and not of the Indians. What was the intention of the British to appoint poorly paid and desperately illiterate police officers/ men to perform police powers under the Code of Criminal Procedure - 1861? - and certainly, the purpose was not at all to administer full justice to Indians. How could they question suspects? How could they search a house, prepare a scene mahazar, register a criminal case or record a witness statement with their ignorance? They were not given any academic or intellectual training. They were put to strenuous physical training which could make them robust men with an army-men like attitude to Indians. The result was abuse of authority or misuse of power in favour of the British rulers. The British utilitarianism - the British self-interest only could be seen in their policing strategies in India. Police becomes a meaningful service not at all when it involves in an egoistic pursuit of pleasure but when it performs duties with an altruistic attitude for the common good–with a genuine concern for the removal of injustice/miscarriage of justice. Police must find pleasure in rendering service to all people - in a human rights friendly way - for administering just justice. One becomes disturbed when he sees the evils in police administration.

Pessimism in Police Administration

Arthur Schopenhauer (1788-1860) was a German philosopher and he was a pessimist. His philosophy and outlook had a decisive influence on English people. Some philosophers defined man as a rational animal, but Schopenhauer said that it was not correct. He agreed that the *reason* might well be man's most valuable possession. He believed that a man would make some pretense of being rational and intelligent and it was to maintain his prestige with other human beings. Sometimes, man did so just to impress upon people who were inferior and at other times to deceive oneself. He thought that beneath all such rational reflection, there was a *dominant will*.

All the Acts which were enforced in India by the British had high sounding objectives. In the Preamble of the Police Act-1861, the British wrote: "whereas it is expedient to reorganize the police and to make it a more efficient instrument for the prevention and detection of crime it is enacted as follows". But, later years saw how efficient was the police in India after the enactment of the Police Act-1861? As Schopenhauer said, it was an act of self-deception and deception of others. The Royal Proclamation of 1858 declared: "*We hold ourselves bound to the natives of our Indian territories by the same obligation of duties which bind us to all our other subjects. In their prosperity will be our strength, in their contentment our security; and in their gratitude our best reward*". The great hopes aroused by the said Proclamation vanished into thin air and Lord Lytton once said: "*We all know that these claims and expectations never can or will be fulfilled*" It was almost like that the Preamble was written in the Police Act-1861. The British knew that the Preamble contained only nice words which were empty utterances. The Police Commission: 1902-03 wrote: "*the police force is far from efficient; it is defective in training and organization; it is inadequately supervised; it is generally regard as corrupt and oppressive; and it has utterly failed to secure the confidence and cordial cooperation of the people*". What more one needed to say that the Preamble of the Police Act-1861 contained only empty words and hollow hopes? The same Police Act-1861 is in force even today and certainly such as Act can ensure only *wounded justice*. The Commission wrote: "Everywhere the Commission heard the most bitter complaints of the corruption of the police.... By officials of all classes including Magistrates and police officers, both European and Native....the police system seems....to have aggravated the evil both by underpaying the constable and by assigning to him duties which he is not qualified to perform....It is urgently necessary to remove any excuse for dishonesty which Government should never allow to exist, by giving to the constable a living wage and reasonable means of supporting himself and family without resort to dishonest practices....The strongest complaints are made in the country regarding the beat system and regarding the permission too frequently given to constables to investigate cases, and in the towns regarding the powers of constables in references to nuisance cases....frequent are the complaints of the highhanded indifference of police here to the feelings of the people....(and) the coarse and brutal way in which the police often treat crowds or individuals with whom they have to deal. This is alleged everywhere as a cause of police unpopularity, as a reason for the people dreading the police and making every effort to avoid having anything to do with them....".

Where was the Preamble of the Police Act-1861? What was happening at the ground level? Was it wounded justice? or miscarriage of justice? or injustice? Look at the prevailing situation now - i.e., after a century since the Police Commission: 1902-03 expressed their view - and one may see that the wounded justice/miscarriage of justice/injustice continues to rule the atmosphere.

The British after writing an enviable Preamble to the Indian Police Act-1861 wanted to see that the police were used to keep the people of the Country effectively and powerfully repressed. Certainly they became successful in their attempts, but after India's independence in 1947, it becomes very difficult for the police to act as a repressive force in a democracy. Schopenhauer says: "People are often reproached for wishing for money above all things, and for loving it more than anything else; but it is natural and even inevitable for people to love that which, like an unwearied Proteus, is always ready to turn itself into whatever object their wandering wishes or their manifold desires may fix upon. Everything else can satisfy only one wish; money alone is absolutely good, ...because it is the abstract satisfaction of every wish". The British wanted money, fortune, power, rule, authority, exploitation etc. and they created a police force. They never made any attempts to turn into joy - into the joy of the people for whom the police force was created. Again to quote Schopenhauer : "Men are a thousand times more intent on becoming rich than on acquiring culture, though it is quite certain that what a man is contributes more to his happiness than what he has". This is what happened to India even after India became independent. The police contributed more to their happiness than what they have for others. They could not become cultured and the results were acquisition of wealth for some of them and administration of *wounded justice* to the people.

Seventeenth Century Europe - that was a time which is customarily called the age of reason. Rene Descartes (1596-1650) and Benedict Spinoza (1632-1677) had their contributions during this period. Rationalism - a philosophy came into being. Spinoza, more over, was very much committed to the political ideals of democracy and freedom. Spinoza is often called the founder of the philosophy of political liberalism. He wrote: "Doomed indeed is any land where opinions are put on trial and condemned as crimes, and where those who avow them are sacrificed, not to public safety, but to the hatred and savagery of their enemies. Deeds alone should be made grounds of criminal charges and speech should be utterly free. Every man should be allowed to think what he likes and to say what he thinks; without such freedom there can not be any peace or true piety". Will Durant in his *The Story of Philosophy* says that the influences of Spinoza rose on the tide of the Revolutionary movement in England. But when England became an imperialistic country, they did not respect the views held by Spinoza. A close scrutiny of the provisions contained in the Indian Penal Code - 1860, the Code of Criminal Procedure - 1861,the Indian Evidence Act-1872 and the Police Act of 1861 would show that the British never wanted to respect the Indian views/opinions and they wanted to administer criminal justice with their brute force by causing fear of police among the people.

The powers of arrest, methods of interrogation, procedure of search, treating of people in police custody etc. were of such a nature that the police could be considered more as a brute force than as an agency to administer justice to Indians. The legislations enacted for Indians were passed by a council composed entirely of Europeans. The views and opinions of Indians were not taken into account. Sir Bartle Frere wrote in the Minute dated 16-03-1860 that Indians ought to be included in Legislative Councils and their opinions ought to be respected. He wrote : "the *perilous* experiment of continuing to legislate for millions of people with few means of knowing, except by rebellion, whether the laws suit them or not" was to be done away with. But, that was of no use then. The brute force created by the British legislations continued to tyranize the society. The Indian Police Commission: 1902-03 wrote: "The Commission can not resist the strong testimony as to the prevalence of corruption among station - house officers throughout the country....It manifests itself in every stage of work of the police station. The police officer may levy a fee or receive a present for every duty he performs. The complainant has often to pay a fee for having his complaint recorded. He has to give the investigating officer a present to secure his prompt and earnest attention to the case. More money is extorted as the investigation proceeds....People are harassed...sometimes by having to accompany him from place to place, sometimes by attendance at the police station....sometimes by threats of evil consequences to themselves and to their friends (especially to the woman of the family) if they do not fall in with his view of the case, sometimes by invasion of their houses by low caste people on the plea of searching for property....From all this deliverance is often to be brought only be payment of fees or presents in cash. The station house officer will sometimes hush up a case on payment of his terms, he will receive presents from parties and their witnesses; he will levy illicit fees from shopkeepers and others for services rendered; or to obviate vexatious espionage. He has a specially rich vein in cases concerning disputes about land, water or crops....". These were the realities that happened in the administration of wounded justice prior to 1900 in India and recent studies conducted by K.S. Sukla too showed the same state of affairs in police service. The study report (1974) writes: "A significant group of witnesses stated that they were obliged by the police to accompany them from place to place and about 22 per cent of them stated that they had to accompany the police to the police stations. Of these, about 25 per cent stated that they were called once, about 14 per cent twice, about 5 per cent thrice and about 6 per cent more than three times. About 20 per cent of the witnesses indicated that they were threatened by the police. About 12 per cent of the witnesses stated that the police threatened them that they would be arrested and their family members harassed, if they did not state something according to the wishes of the police....The general conclusion that could be drawn from this is that the experience of a large number of witnesses with the police and with the entire legal profession in general is so unsatisfactory that they would try to avoid getting involved in the same again as far as possible or will do so only with the greatest reluctance". The question is : "What is the difference between the police in India during 1900 and during 1974?" Another question is "Has the police changed now during 2000?" A third question is: "Is it administration of justice or administration of wounded justice?" What the Torture Commission said in 1855 is repeated by all State Police Commissions and National Police Commission (1977-81) and the situation continues as it was even today (?) This shows that the administration of wounded justice has a history of nearly two centuries in India. The enduring significance of Spinoza's thoughts which were widely recognized in England had no impact in India when the British reorganized the police and enacted legislations to administer criminal justice. They wanted to repress the Indians and they did everything for that purpose and the police was a weapon for the purpose. Most unfortunately, the same laws which made the police a weapon and a coercive force for the British imperialism continue to rule the country even after 50 years of freedom. What a tragedy!

Hedonism, Police and Wounded Justice

Epicurus (341-270 B.C.) wrote: "Pleasure is our first and kindred good. It is the starting point of every choice and every aversion, and to it we come back and make feeling the rule by which to judge of every good thing....Wherefore we call pleasure the Alpha and Omega of a blessed life". This is called the philosophy of *hedonism*. Pleasures can be of many types. Police service is created for establishing and sustaining the pleasure of having law and order in society by preventing crimes and by administering justice. The British did not have this in their mind. They wanted a repressive police force to keep the Indians under their deterrent control. The objective of the police system was stated to be "to make the police a more efficient instrument for prevention and detection of crimes". But, the British wanted the objectives to be fulfilled by repressive tactics and they enacted laws for the same. How could such a force be people-friendly? How could such a force be human rights friendly? How could such a force administer fair justice? The British were not concerned about such delicate issues. They did not think about Magna Carta and its contents when they enacted criminal legislations in India.

The Indian Penal Code contained 23 chapters with 511 sections. Transportation was a punishment then and the same was dropped in England. Penal servitude was substituted for transportation for Europeans. There were criticisms that the Code provided wide scope for police officers for malpractices. They could register a case under a serious penal section or under a light penal section. There were as many as thirteen sections in house tresspass, five in theft, three in robbery and seven in dacoity. A simple hurt could be registered as an attempt to murder. If the police wanted, they could interpret any human behavior as a violation of the penal law and could find out cognizable sections to register even non-cognizable cases.

There were allegations against the police that they enforced the penal law with a hedonistic attitude. They derived sensual pleasures by doing thus! The Indian Police Commission: 1902-03 wrote: "The Commission have received endless narrations of the worries involved in a police investigation. A body of police comes down to the village and is quartered on it for several days. The principal residents have to dance attendance on the police all day long and for days together. Sometimes, all the villagers are compelled to be in attendance, and inquiries degrading in their character are conducted *coram populo*. Suspects and innocent persons are bullied and threatened into giving information they are supposed to possess. The police officer, owing to want of detective ability or to indolence, directs his efforts to procure confessions by improper inducements, by threats or by moral pressure....Sometimes suspects, whom the police officer does not desire to report as under arrest, are kept for days together under so-called 'surveillance' which is nothing else than unauthorized confinement or restraint, a system which affords serious opportunity for malpractices". Why did the police do so during the British raj? Was it with an intention to make the police efficient for investigation and detection of crime? Or, was it for deriving an Epicurean pleasure? Epicureanism, in common usage, defines Oxford Dictionary of Philosophy, is "a way of life based on sensual enjoyment". If the police did all those things as narrated by the Police Commission: 1902-03, then there was an element of sensual pleasure which could be considered only as an administration of wounded justice.

Could the police do anything in the pretext of administering criminal justice? The Police Commission: 1902-03 again writes:

"All this is done to secure evidence in support of the view which the police officer from time to time holds regarding the case. If in his opinion, enough evidence is not thus obtained to secure a conviction, he will not hesitate to bloster up his case with false evidence. Sometime this leads to an innocent person being prosecuted through police mistakes. More often perhaps it leads to guilty persons escaping through the suspicion thrown on the police evidence. Many a good case has been ruined in this way; but the police officer is unduly impelled by the statistical test to try to make his investigation fails, the complainant is sometimes finally bullied or threatened into acknowledging that a mistake has been made, and that the case is 'false'. When it is successful, the accused is often subjected to unnecessary annoyance; the law about bail is overlooked; the rules limiting the use of handcuff are forgotten; and so serious effort is made to treat the accused with that consideration as to his food and comfort to which....he is entitled until he is convicted".

British sense of justice — that has become a sacred saying among the Indian lawyers and if this was what the British police did in the name of administering justice, then it was not wounded justice—rather was gross and crude injustice to the poor people in this great Country.

The police are now in the 21st century - in the third millennium and we are confronted today with the same crisis in justice administration as the crisis we had about a century ago. Before 1900, the wounded justice was administered by the police in the British raj and today, it is being done and perpetuated by the Indian police in people's rule. What a tragedy indeed! The basic values of human existence as we conceive them - i.e., man's right to get fair justice, just justice, full justice, equal justice, gender justice enforcement justice, human rights justice, social justice, victim justice etc - are being subjected to such increasing restraint today that people's very rights to desire for just justice seems threatened by police misdoings or their administration of wounded justice. This, I do not think, is not a crisis which can be solved by innovations and development of science and technology or by globalization or any such "*....lizations*". What we face today is an existential crisis-a crisis that concerns the very nature and meaning of justice administration. And for this reason it is a situation in which criminologists, jurists, legislators, judges, police officers and all those who love justice and justice administration should find out significant solution. People have been suffering wounded justice administration for centuries and they can not tolerate it any longer. The worth of the individual must have to be recognized and the dignity of man ought to have to be respected.

3

Wounded Justice: The Police Legacy or People's Curse?

Some people in a village believed that the sun was devoured by a snake by name *Raahu* during solar eclipse and they could not tolerate it. Hence, they used to keep a good stick with them for the purpose of killing the snake - Raahu - during the eclipse. What they did was that they used to beat on the earth with the stick and it continued till the eclipse was over. Certainly, they had misconceptions about the solar eclipse and they sincerely thought that the snake ought to be killed. Now, most of the people in that village do not do anything to kill the snake. For, they know the scientific explanations of solar eclipse and they know that the snake has nothing to do with the Sun. Nevertheless, the old women in that village take a fragile splinter-like thin stick with them and start beating the snake, and they do it without it being taken note of by others. Why do they do so? Their answer is: "The mind is restless unless and until we do it". O.K., let them do so as long as they want it. But, people who know the scientific explanation of solar eclipse may say that their misconceptions or superstitions work deeply there and they have to be educated about the scientific aspect of solar eclipse. The story of the wounded justice too is almost like this. The British enacted the laws and the people did not know what the laws were. Police enforced the law and the people believed that the way they enforced the laws was the way justice ought to be executed. The police functionaries who executed the laws, the Indian Police Commission: 1902-03 wrote, "were men deficient in education and intelligence". The Commission used the words "*ignorant and inefficient*" head constables. The Commission observed "dishonesty among the supervisory ranks in police". Even about the superintendents of police the Commission wrote: "that they are often not well educated or intelligent men, that their training is defective, that their knowledge of the vernacular is not such as to enable them to have free intercourse with the people and to become acquainted with their feelings and circumstances, that they are too much in the hands of their subordinates, that they are not accessible or even courteous to natives, that their views are too narrow and their sense of responsibility too weak to allow them to pay due regard to complaints against their subordinates or strictures on their work or to take due notice of misconduct, that they are too burdened with clerical work and too little helped by qualified assistants to be able to exercise effective supervision and control over the police". What type of justice they would have ensured and enforced to the people? Needless to say that the people suffered them and suffered them as they had no other option. Some ignorant and illiterate people honestly thought that they received justice from police and certainly they had only misconceived concepts of justice. Like the villagers who killed the snake which was supposed to devour the Sun, the illiterate and ignorant people in India lived in a world which had only misconceived ideas about justice and justice administration. A few who knew the extent and intensity of injustice done to the people in the pretext of administering justice did not react to the miscarriage of justice by police. Many people were afraid of the police and some of them encouraged the police to commit atrocities on people. As the old story goes, the king was naked, but nobody said anything about it - rather praised the king until, at least the child uttered: "Look, the king is naked".

Ideal Justice, Just Justice and Wounded Justice

Justice must be rational - this was what the Indians missed during the British raj. Rational is real and the rational only will last and that is what the people of India want to achieve now in justice administration. People want justice and they want real and rational justice. People today are not prepared to accept anything as justice and the *interpreted justice* by police often do not get public approval. "We use third degree methods on property offenders and recidivists because they deserve them and the people want them to be used" - said a police officer and his interpreted justice was summarily rejected by the international community which proclaimed a Convention Against Torture. A study of the concept of justice the people had might prove that it was nothing but their interest in the case and as an agency enjoying power and authority, they executed things in the way they wanted. Sometimes it was wounded justice and at other times, it was miscarriage of justice or injustice proper. The British did not want to employ the natives in offices of trust as they thought that it would be the beginning of the end for the British empire in India. It may be reiterated emphatically what the Secretary of State in British India said: "It should never be forgotten, and there should never be any hesitation in laying down the principle, that it is one of our first duties to the people of India to guard the safety of our own dominion....the maintenance and stability of our rule must ever be kept in view as the basis of our police, and to this end large proportions of British functionaries in the more important posts seen essential". All the legislations they passed were intended to safeguard their interests first and then to protect the interests of Indians. The police thus was first to protect the British interests and administration of justice, by whatever way via police was of secondary importance for them. The British treated the lowest rank as unskilled labourers and paid them a pay equal to such labourers. They wanted one policemen to every 5 square miles (1 mile=1.609 kilometer) and for every 1000 inhabitants. It meant that they did not want better qualified people to aid the administration of justice. It could be said that the justice these policemen could ensure was the unskilled labourers' justice to the people. When the police force was formed, it contained literate, semi-literate and illiterate constables who could just read and write. What type of justice could they offer to people? This was not the concern of the British. They had their self-interests and they did many things including an administration of *wounded justice*-miscarriage of justice-injustice and the salaries of the constables in the reorganized Bengal police in three grades were Rs 6, Rs.7 and Rs.8 and the salary of the inspector general of police was Rs.3000. The Rs.5 police constable who could just read and write did not understand the provisions of law in the Indian Penal Code, Code of Criminal Procedure, Police Act, Indian Evidence Act etc and the Rs.3000 British police inspector general utilized or misused them as *Animal Men* to administer justice which was to their advantage. All legislations were enacted and robust *Animal Men* were employed in order to make their rule smooth. *A good police service* - that was not their concern at all; rather, they wanted a *brutal police force* and they succeeded in creating one. A policeman growing up in an atmosphere which administers *wounded justice* naturally and inevitably develops an entirely different outlook on justice and the methods of administering justice from that of a policeman who grows up in an environment which ensures administration of just justice. The British did not provide an atmosphere for policemen for developing a sense of just justice during their rule in India. The police could not do what was just and fair simply by following the British approved laws and standards. They failed to understand that justice was not guaranteed just by applying a set of rules in a crude or barbarous way by policemen on people's acts. The way or the manner in which the rules were applied did matter a lot, but that was not the police or British concern in India at that time. The policemen themselves were found to involve themselves in the commission of crimes. Anandswarup Gupta in his book 'The Police in British India: 1881-1947' writes: "some policemen in Gaya district were found to have been busily engaged for years in the commission of dacoities, mail robberies, and other offences, with the chief object of gaining a reputation for detective ability for securing the conviction of innocent persons for crimes which they themselves had committed or caused to be committed. He continues: "Some policemen were suspected to be in corrupt connivance with dacoits among the *Bheels*, 200 of whom were captured and convicted in 1880. The police of Nimar were reported to have proved very inefficient and it was said that an all-round improvement was needed in the investigation of crimes. The percentage of convictions declined which was reported to be unsatisfactory". The same situation existed during 1880 continues even today during 2000 AD as one finds that the conviction rate is deplorably low. Large number of acquittals is indicative of administration of wounded justice - miscarriage of justice - injustice proper. Democracy has been in existence in India for more than 50 years and the administration of *wounded justice* continues to rule the Country. John Dewey (1859-1952) wrote long ago: "In a democracy we often make mistakes. We fail to act promptly and decisively when we should. We frequently elect the wrong men to public office and we tolerate both stupidity and graft on the part of our public officials". Is this observation true in the case of administration of *wounded justice* in Indian democracy? The Penal Code prescribed very severe penalties for offences, but the conviction rate was not enviable in British India and it continues to be the same even today. Why?

In Calcutta Review (No. 157,1884), it was written: "there was not much complaint against the spread of violent crime as against the existing protective organization". It indicated the people's dissatisfaction about police performance and a low estimation of what the police were doing then. The Review continued: "The disrepute and unpopularity of the police is undoubtedly a very frequent cause of its demoralization. It is curious that a service which exists ostensibly for the benefit of the public, should stand so low in public estimation....In India, there were special reasons for the bad odour which attaches itself to the very word *police*. The force is invested with enormous powers, and paid at inadequate rates of salary, and at the same time very little care is exercised in the selection of candidates for the various posts". Has the situation improved to the better now? If not, administration of *wounded justice* will be the result in any case. The Calcutta Review says further: "The police officer, when once appointed, has ordinarily little to fear in the way of really efficient supervision, and, as a natural consequence, he too often systematically preys on the people from the date of his appointment to that of retirement. This alone would be enough to make the service unpopular with the best class of natives....The best appointment constantly fall to low caste men, who have, as such, far greater powers for evil than an aristocratic incumbent would possess because of the injury they can inflict on any high caste person who should happen to offend them; and, besides, from the accident of their birth they are retained by no sanctions and no considerations of any kind from making their appointment as lucrative as possible.... The police are usually useless, that is, they are paid by the State for no appreciable services to the community or else they are a positive evil". How has the position bettered today?

Police service is maintained for administering just justice and thereby to achieve what is best in human life and best for human welfare. This is particularly true in a democracy and precisely therefore it is felt that the police service must be marked by a greater sensitiveness to social well-being through fair administration of just justice. They have to recognize and respect human values, morality and true humanism. Police with a conscience - enforcement of law with a conscience - administration of just justice with an upright conscience - they must be the guiding force of police for the third millennium. They must have human values that lie behind them. Belief in man-oriented police service and in moral responsibility through an upright conscience appears to be very essential for policemen/ officers to administer justice to people. The police in India lacked this consciousness even in the British Raj. The Commissioner of Lucknow said in 1888 that the police were a disreputable body and they knew it; they were therefore, mistrusted and hampered even when they wished to work openly and fairly. To it, the Senior Commissioner in the same province added: "Every year convinces me that....the police are honey combed with corruption. Facts constantly come to my knowledge which convince me of this, although it would be hard to prove them in a judicial inquiry". The same view is expressed by many police officers, politicians, publicmen and the press even today. Is it a curse for Indian police that they do not come up to the expectations of the public? The opinions expressed by the participants of a seminar recently show:

(1) The detection rate of crimes is very low

(2) The conviction rate is deplorably low

(3) There is corruption at all levels - wider and higher

(4) The police use unauthorized methods during interrogation.

(5) There are human rights violations during investigations of crimes.

(6) Enforcement criminality is seen in many areas

(7) There is victimization and abuse of power/misuse of authority.

(8) There is lack of police - public cooperation and vice versa.

(9) The policemen including senior levels are ignorant of laws and procedure.

(10) Scientific investigation is lacking and the crude methods are objectionable.

(11) There is concoction of evidence in criminal cases.

(12) Manipulation of records, production of false witnesses, tutoring of witnesses take place.

(13) There is lack of cooperation between police and prosecuting agencies.

(14) They mismanage investigation and misinform courts.

(15) There is suppression of facts or suggestion of falsehood during trial.

(16) Registering of false cases takes place for victimization.

(17) The standard of quality and intelligence of investigating officers are at best suspicious.

(18) Police become vulnerable to influences and political pressures.

(19) They act vindictively to politicians for making political advantage to the ruling party.

(20) There is lack of supervision and many superior ranks lack information on supervision.

(21) There is lack of human formation in police service. They fail to/refuse to enforce law with an upright human conscience.

(22) Many are poor in scriptory work and some senior officers lack knowledge in vernacular and culture of the people.

(23) Some have inflated ego and vanities of police uniform.

(24) Work culture is lacking and discipline is disrupted.

(25) Interpersonnel hostility and clashes take place.

And thus, one may see any number of such negative aspects which lead but to *wounded justice*. No doubt, the concern of the police functionaries during the millennium must be to increase scientific knowledge and the scientists' devotion to duty and truth. The police must be human rights friendly and should possess an upright conscience and human formation.

Immanuel Kant (1724-1804) said that *every man should understand the nature of morality* in his work. For that he must begin with "the pure, unspoiled moral mind of man". No doubt, the influence of the police sub-culture may corrupt a policeman. The period of induction training and a few years of service in police sub-culture may be enough to play havoc with such simple, unspoiled moral convictions of a young officer in police service. They must therefore go back to that simple and unsophisticated moral conviction which they believe everyone in society possesses. This alone can help to avoid *wounded justice* administration in the present set-up. About the unspoiled moral outlook, Immanuel Kant writes that "*one can be good if he wants to*". Not all police officers can become a scientific investigator, a successful manager of law and order or an intelligent collector of intelligence. But, certainly, they can become good if they want to. To quote Kant again: "Something in the world, it says, are doubtless destined to be enjoyed only by the gifted and the privileged. Whether we shall be happy, influential, successful, or what not, depends always to a great extent on matters beyond our control - on natural gifts, inherited temperament, congenial circumstances". But, I think that it is not so of every accomplishment in police. There is one achievement that is open to an ordinary policeman as it is to the director general of police. I agree with Immanuel Kant who says: "*only in certain circumstances can you be happy; but you can always be good*. This is one hundred per cent applicable in police work, for, to be good in police work, one needs only" to want to be so". If the policeman wholly wants to be good, then he is so.

But, history does not show such policemen in large numbers. The reports of the Indian Police Commission: 1902-03, State Police Commissions hitherto appointed, National Police Commission: 1977-81 and research studies bear testimony to the above facts. What went wrong here? Some policemen want to do what is just and right; but they become confused as to what is just and right. The police sub-culture tells them what is just and right, but their own conscience does not permit them to do things as taught by the police sub-culture. The customs, conventions, unwritten laws of practice, traditions etc. which form the police sub-culture make them to do many things in an unethical or illegal or unlawful manner. Unless the moral convictions of the policemen is quite strong, he is very likely to accept a position of moral *relativism* and adopts some purely personal standards to guide his conduct. He may then say that he is right according to police standards. He may bring the concept of *professional ethics*, and he may justify anything the police do unethically. For him, use of torture, epithets, filthy language etc. are quite acceptable and he does not think that all such undesirable strategies are nothing but manifestations of *wounded justice*.

Moral Relativism in Police

Read Torture Commission Report-1855, Indian Police Commission Reports: 1902-03, National Police Commission Reports: 1977-81, news papers, periodicals, research reports, judgements from law courts and one may see a number of unethical acts done by police inside, outside or both of their job. Why do they do so? What are their justifications? I have asked these questions to many policemen/officers and they have been speaking the same things from 1976 (when I joined the police service) till now. I have noted that they have been more emotional than rational in their responses. I have further noted that they have no convincing answers to the questions. I used to ask myself: "Do these people have guilt feelings for what they do?" I have found out an answer for my question. Those who justify their illegal acts suffer from *moral relativism*. I have noticed that some of them are unable to convince themselves about the morality of their unethical police acts although they speak loudly about the justifiability of their unethical acts. In some, I have seen real conflicts - conflicts between their *superego* and their acts. Those who have a strong moral background will condemn their unethical act and those who have a weak moral background will be indifferent to their unethical acts. Those who are in between the strong and the weak moral background attempt to justify their unethical acts under *moral relativism*. They become skeptical about what is right and what is wrong.

Police use of torture or their degrading, cruel behavior etc. may be the offshoot of their experience in the past. They might have had success through these shortcuts in police work and thus they made such unethical strategies parts of the police culture. Can we call it an *empirical morality* which according to Immanuel Kant is nothing but relative and subject to change. In any police act, there is an empirical content and also three is a rational content. The rational content is universal and it recognizes no borders. Human rights laws may form the rational content of police act and it comes from a policeman's sense of obligation to what is right and what is wrong in police job. The policemen ought to do his duties, no matter what may be the consequences. The police in India failed to do so and that was the precise reason why they were criticized everywhere. They did things according to their self-interest or being pressured by forces beyond their control. They did not give any importance to the ethical content in their actions.

Wounded justice - is it a moral evil or a legal evil? It is both and therefore *legal relativism* and *empirical legality* are the same as *moral relativism* and *empirical morality* as far as wounded justice is concerned. Provisions are seen in the Indian

Penal Code and Code of Criminal Procedure against the use of torture, coercion, force or undue influence during police interrogation. Yet, the police employ them and if that is the truth, then they violate the rational content of legality. This is the reason why the use of force etc. (wounded justice) by police is condemned everywhere.

How can the police avoid the dangers of legal relativism and build a legality that is valid for everyone, everywhere regardless of circumstances? The police in India never raised this question - rather have been trying to rationalize their illegal acts. In order to build a legality that is valid, the police have to get away from anything that is based on their experience or training. According to Immanuel Kant, they must derive their principles entirely from a legal a *priori*, the *categorical imperative* of duty. Kant says: "Always act on that maxim. which can at the same time be made a universal law of conduct". The maxims are given in the international covenants on human rights and in the Constitution of India and also in the laws made thereunder. In British India, the Constitution of India was not in existence, nevertheless, there were legal maxims and provisions in law. The police in India just ignored them and one reason for that was their ignorance of the laws of the land. There were literature and illiterate constables in the British raj and what good would come from such ignorant people for administration of justice!

4

Wounded Justice:

The Police Pragmatism or People's Fatalism?

"Suppose, your sister is molested and raped. How will you investigate the case? Will you use third degree methods to get a confession from the suspect?" - asked a police officer to a human rights activist. Of course, it was a personal question and necessarily, emotions were involved.

A judge in a High Court lost Rs. 10,000 and he had suspected a certain person. He told the police investigator: "you question the suspect in the police way" and he meant to employ torture on the suspect. These and similar situations arise during police work and then, what to do? There is a school of thought which argues that torture, cruel and degrading treatments become necessary and inevitable at times in police work. Theoretically they can not be employed, but in practice, the police can not but make use of them. People who do not go to a war field can speak many things about how to fight a war. But, the actual soldier can not fight a war in the way moralists, philosophers and theologians tell about it. Likewise, the human rights activists can preach on human rights of suspects, arrestees, accused and so on. But, they do not face the live situations. The cow in the book does not eat grass! Investigation of crime is always a practical matter. The major issue which the police face is the conflict of good and evil in crime investigation.

William James (1842-1910) a philosopher of pragmatism says: "Every man must act as he thinks best; and if he is wrong, so much the worse for him. We stand on a mountain pass in the midst of whirling snow and blinding mist, through which we get glimpses now and then of paths which may be deceptive. If we stand still we shall be frozen to death. If we take the wrong road we shall be dashed to piece. We do not certainly know whether there is any right one. What must we do? *Be strong and of a good courage.* Act for the best, hope for the best and take what comes". If this philosophy is taken, then the police argument that violation of human rights becomes inevitable and necessary in certain cases ceases to have any meaning. For, one must act for the best, hope for the best and take what comes. What is best is to be decided on the basis of principles set by the society and law. The history of police in India shows that the police failed to perform their duties as per law. Wrongly interpreted *pragmatism* guided their activities. In the beginning of 20th century, the inspector general of police, Madras wrote in the Administration Report of 1904: "Since 1900, there has been on the whole a steady and continuous decrease in the success of the police in bringing evil-doers to punishment.... Always unpopular, the department has become more than ever an easy, and as it were an authorized target for aspersion both in the press and in the courts....with diminished credit and prestige, the influence of the police has declined throughout the country and the respect in which it was held, has decreased, with the inevitable further result of diminished efficiency".

A casual reading of the report of the Indian Police Commission: 1902-03 may reveal that the police in India involved themselves in all kinds of malpractices and corruption. The observations of the inspector general of police further substantiated the Police Commission's views and one could not agree with policemen/officers who advocated human rights violations in the name of pragmatism. It would then be administration of wounded justice.

The police must do everything as per law and by the procedure established by law. Not only that they must do their work in the way stated above, they also must do things with a conscience which is legal as well as moral. There must not be two accounts in police work - one for writing those things which are legally done and another for writing those things which are morally done. Police have only one account book and it must contain legal acts done with a moral sense having an upright conscience. Pragmatism must not be misinterpreted to mean anything the police do according to their whims and fancies. Any police action has its consequences. If the consequences are damaging to the administration of justice, then there is no meaning in speaking about pragmatic philosophy. As it is today from what it has been during the last century till yesterday, one may see that the pragmatism of police through illegal and unauthorized methods has never yielded to carve out a good image of the police service. This is the view the press, media and researchers have on police today. It was so in the past as well. Sir Edmund Cox (in 1910) wrote that the recommendations of the Police Commission: 1902-03 did not make any difference in police behavior. He continued: "when a crime has been committed in a village, the police investigation that ensures is likely in the nature of things to cause annoyance to a number of people....If the accused are well-to-do people, they are always ready to offer bribes to the police to hush the charge up. The charges of bribe-taking, usually made in anonymous or pseudonymous letters are incessant. Sometimes they are true, in others they are certainly false". What Cox said in 1910 is true even today and it shows that the history of wounded justice administration is very old in Indian sub-continent.

Investigation, the police say emphatically, is a probe to find out the truth. What is truth and how must it be probed into? The police may say that something is the truth and is it true to say that *that truth* is the *real truth*? If that is the real truth, then the police can resort to honest and true methods to probe into and prove the truth. Do the police do so? Or, have they ever done it in police history? They have and they have not and their *have nots* are published in the press and media.

Will the High Court judge ask a police officer to question the suspect in the *police way* if the suspect happens to be his wife or son? No doubt, emotions are involved and the pragmatism may take a different course of action altogether. Likewise, if the rapist happens to be the police investigator's own father or his only brother, will the police officer have recourse to third degree methods? In all probability, the pragmatism may search for other methods. Truth must be found out and the methods used to find out the truth must also be just, fair and true. Instances are not rare that innocent people have been tortured to plead guilty. This obnoxious practice was in existence even before the report of the Torture Commission - 1855 was published. The N.W.P. Police Committee (1911 AD) commended the Bombay Rules on the action to be taken against those police officers who employed torture. These rules provided that severe notice should be taken of the ill-treatment of accused persons by the police and that prosecution should be instituted where necessary. They laid down that:, "directly an accused person is placed under arrest, the investigating police officer shall, as the first step in the police investigation, ask him whether he has any complaint to make of ill-treatment by the police and shall enter in the case-diary the question and answer. If an allegation of ill-treatment is made, the investigating officer shall there and then examine the prisoner's body, if the prisoner consents, to see if there are any marks of ill-treatment and to record the result of his examination. If the prisoner refuses to allow his body to be examined, the refusal and the reasons therefore shall be recorded. If the investigating officer finds that there is reason to believe the allegation of ill-treatment, he shall at once, so far suspend the investigation on which the prisoner has been arrested as to forward the prisoner with his complaint, the record of corporal examination, any other evidence available, and, if possible, the police officer implicated by the prisoner's complaint, to the nearest magistrate having jurisdiction to enquire into the case". In 1911, the police officers were permitted to conduct corporal examination of the arrestees and now the Supreme Court of India, in D.K. Basu Vs. State of West Bengal authorizes only qualified medical officer to examine the body of the arrestee. It shows that there is distrust on police examination and more trust on a medical examination conducted by a qualified medical officers. In practice, it is always difficult to get the service of a medical officer to conduct the corporal examination, yet the Supreme Court favors only such an examination. It may be to ensure that the body examination is conducted by qualified people and not by police officers. To conclude one may say that the arguments, from *pragmatism* and rationalization of unauthorized acts which the police do during crime-investigation, are nothing but symptoms of wounded justice administration. If the police *hearts* do not want to administer fair and just justice, then the police *heads* will never make them to administer just justice. Police is a good service - a desirable service - only when it does something good for the individual and society. The common man goes to police only when he is convinced that he will get justice, but many people avoid police, for they are afraid that they will get only wounded justice in case they go closer to police.

God is Dead, Justice is Wounded

Friedrich Nietzsche (1844 - 1900) gives a parable in *The Gay Science* - a book written by him. The parable is:

The Mad Man

Have you not heard of that mad man who lit a lantern on the bright morning hours, ran to the market place, and cried incessantly: "I seek God! I seek God!" As many as those who did not believe in God were standing around just then, he provoked much laughter. Why did he get lost? Said one - Or, is he hiding? Is he afraid of us? Has he gone on a voyage? Or emigrated? Thus, they yelled and laughed.

The mad man jumped into their mist and pierced them with his glances. "Whither is God", he cried. "I shall tell you. We have killed him – you and I. All of us are his murderers....Whither are we moving now? Away from all suns?....Are we not straying as through an infinite nothing? Do we not feel the breath of empty space? Has it not become colder? Is not night and more night coming on all the while?

God is dead! God remains dead. And we have killed him. What was holiest and most powerful of all that the world has yet owned has bled to death under our knives. Who will wipe this blood off?

Here the mad man fell silent and looked again at his listeners; and they too were silent and stared at him in astonishment. At last he threw his lantern on the ground, and it broke and went out. "I have come too early"- he said then; my time has not yet come. This tremendous even is still on its way– it has not yet reached the ears of man".

This parable told by Nietzsche may be applicable to the *Wounded justice* administered to people. "God is dead"–says Nietzsche and "justice is wounded"–say the people and the history so far. A pamphlet titled 'Police Reforms" from Dinsha Edulji Wacha from Allahabad in 1911 said about the police: "The rotten organization which purported to protect life and property and detect true crimes" and a High Court Judge from Allahabad said just recently that there was no organized group of criminals in the whole country whose record of crime would come any way near to the record of crimes committed by that organized group which was called the Indian police. With the death of God, man's dignity as man is gone and the values which give meaning to his life are gone. If this is what Nietzsche thinks when he confirms that the *God is dead*, the people may say that the justice is dead or wounded justice only is possible for man. What is the relevance and meaning of a mammoth system if it can ensure only wounded justice?

"Mankind is not yet mad only because the death of God has not been discovered"–says Nietzsche emphatically and the people down the centuries feel that they maintain the system because they do not know that the system offers only wounded justice. They have yet to discover that the system can not and does not ensure just justice unless the people who are in system are just, honest and decent. As the God is dead, people wander through an endless nothingness - Nietzsche feels and likewise, as the justice administered is wounded, the people wander through a path hoping that one day they will get justice and this hope against hope is the driving force behind justice administration. Down the centuries, one sees amendments of law and enactments of law for fairer justice to people. This is the hope of the people who maintain the justice system in the world.

Does the End Justify the Means?

It is Karl Marx (1818-1883) who said that the *end justified the means*. The end in every criminal investigation and trial must be punishment for the guilty by a court of law. In some cases, the police may be fully convinced about the involvement of the suspect in a crime, nevertheless, they may be helplessly helpless to prove the crime before a court of law by independent evidence. They may have to, in such instances, create the evidence and then how? Some policemen say that the end of criminal investigation is administration of justice and there is nothing wrong if the police resort to obnoxious practices and to the use of third degree methods etc. For, the end justifies the means. If the end is fine, the means can be foul. This philosophy works deeply among some police investigators and it works as a cause of administering wounded justice without guilt feelings. Historical materialism accepts armed class conflicts, civil war etc. for creating a Maxist society and there every means adopted to reach that classless society is accepted. Likewise, in justice administration too, some police functionaries believe that the end makes everything and there is nothing wrong in having recourse to filthy methods during investigation. Justice loving people may not agree with the argument of such police functionaries as they hold that both the end and means must be just, fair and decent. The communist philosophy had a natural death in many parts of the world and it proved that the philosophy had no survival value. If that is the time proved reality, it is equally true in justice administration too. That is the precise reason why the police are criticized when they adopt human rights unfriendly approaches during their investigation of crimes. During the British Raj, the police did involve in such human atrocities and the repressive police force has been condemned even today. The pamphlet on '*Police Reforms*' mentioned above stated that "Since 1876, the Government have introduced a variety of repressive laws, political and economical, of the strongest character, against which the people have from time to time bitterly inveighed ....The large and repressive laws have been largely contributing to crime and perjury, they have sown the seeds of wide discontentment and stimulated the corruption of the police". It means that the end does not justify the means. Even today, people want just justice through just and human rights friendly means.

All throughout the history of Indian police from 1861, one may note that the efficiency of police in crime investigation and detection or administration of justice was not their concern during the British rule. Training of police officers in crime investigation did not receive any attention. In 1892, a police training school was established at Phillaur, Punjab for the training of sub-inspectors. Even before 1864, police training schools were started at Nagpur and Saugor for the training of inspectors and chief constables, but they were discontinued in 1864. The reason was that they could not spare officers for training. There were some training schools in other parts of the country, but they were intended to give more of physical training to police functionaries. There was no intellectual training worth its name as they mainly wanted physically fit - robust men to repress the Indian masses. One doubts very much whether or not the British wanted to tell them what was meant by justice. Plato (427-347 BC) said: "I proclaim that might is right and justice is the interest of the stronger". Perhaps this was what the constables were taught about justice. The British had their interest in India and they wanted the police to keep up their interest by the help of a repressive force. To quote Plato again: "The different forms of government make laws, democratic, aristocratic or autocratic with a view to their respective interests; and these laws, so made by them, to serve their interests, they deliver to their subjects as *justice* and punish the *unjust* anyone who transgresses them.... I am speaking of injustice on a large scale; and my meaning will be most clearly seen in autocracy, which by fraud and force takes away the property of others, not retail but wholesale. Now, when a man has taken away the money of the citizens and made slaves of them, then, instead of swindler and thief he is called happy and blessed by all. For injustice is censured because those who censure it are afraid of suffering, and not from any scruple they might have of doing injustice themselves".

Administration of justice was not the main concern of the British in India, rather, they wanted it. For, it was a means for them to take away the Indian wealth. They defined theft in the Penal Code and their intention was to catch the petty thieves and they committed theft of the whole country. They defined culpable homicide amounting to murder and not amounting to murder and they murdered a number of Indians who fought against them. They had illiterate and semi-literate Indian constables to work under the white officers and the atrocities they committed were not recorded and therefore one could not know the extent and intensity. What Plato said was true: "I am speaking of injustice on a large scale and my meaning will be most clearly seen in autocracy, which by fraud or force takes away the property of others, not retail but wholesale" and that was what was done by the British in India. They enacted laws and the police was misused as a repressive force for looting or plundering the wealth of the country. They employed the police for quasi-military duties just to suppress the people under one count or another. In 1883, for example, they used the police thus twice in Bengal. Under a nice caption - i.e. to *reestablish public tranquility* - they committed atrocities in India.

Does might make right? - Plato asked and during the British regime, one might see that the might was the right in India and the police and Penal Code etc. were misused to catch the weak and make them their slaves. The British had the power, the force, the army, the police and the determination to plunder the Country. They made laws to catch hold of the Indians who committed thefts, robbery, dacoity etc. so that they could do them without being afraid of anybody. In democratic India, how do the politicians behave? Do they misuse the police strength? Is there any unholy *nexus* between the police and the politicians? Do they misuse the penal laws for their advantage? Aristotle (384-322 BC) said: "For we choose happiness for itself, and never with a view to anything further, whereas we choose honour, pleasure, intellect....because, we believe that through them we shall be made happy". The police has been created by the society as the society wanted to have happiness and harmony through it. But, does the society get it? Though a crimeless or crime-free society is an impossibility, the police can certainly control crimes and thereby maintain peace and happiness. The history from 1860 till today shows that the crimes have been on the increase. In British India, the total crimes increased from 11,21,531 in 1901 to 12,20,283 in 1911 and in free India to 64,11,259 in 1999. The increase is found to be 471.7 per cent. This has to be reckoned with another fact that the police strength has been considerably increased during this period. Could the Indian Society have happiness through police and their ways of administering justice? Police officers are men placed on high positions and they are to administer just justice. Can they do so? Francis Bacon (1561-1626) once said: "Men in great place are thrice servants; servants to the sovereign or State, servants of fame, and servants of business, so as they have no freedom, neither in their person nor in their action, nor in their time....The rising unto place is laborious, and by pains men come to greater pains, and it is sometimes base, and by indignities men come to dignities. The standing is slippery, and the regress is either downfall or atleast an eclipse". The police in the British India were government servants and to the very letter of the words, they were servants of the British Government. They were not free in their persons, actions and time. After India became independent, police officers became public servants. Now, are they free? If press reports are true and believable, then many police officers have been blamed for becoming the servants of the governments in power. As Bacon said: "from indignities men come to dignities. The standing is slippery and the regress is either a downfall or atleast an eclipse". This has been witnessed by the people in some cases and certainly, the blamed officers could administer only *wounded justice*. About wounded justice, Roger Ascham (1515-1568) wrote:

"Cog, lie, flatter and face,

Four ways in Court to win men grace,

If thou be trail to none these,

Away, good Piers! Home, John Cheese!

and that was how he saw the four cardinal virtues in demand at the court of the Queen. He was the tutor of Queen Elizabeth. Has the situation changed now?

If administration of justice was so in England during the period of Roger Ascham in sixteenth century, things were not different in India during the 20th century. The police had to do many things to please the government. The British found that the press made attacks on King Emperor during the beginning of the 20th century and therefore they imposed controls over the press and for it, they misused the police powers. Their repressive policy did not yield results. Repressions resulted in revolution. For example, in 1907, a train carrying the Lieutenant Governor of Bengal (He was the President of the Police Commission) was derailed by a Bomb. In December, 1907, the District Magistrate of Dacca was shot in the back. Even today, the police are attacked by the people. During 1997, a total of 597 police personnel were killed in India; 3832 were injured. Attacks on police personnel on duty are on the increase and the reasons for them must be identified.

Are the police to administer justice? or - to enforce law and order? Today, the police are used for both purposes and therefore there exists a confusion as to what exactly is the role of police in a democracy. Can the law and order police administer fair justice in crime investigation? There is a view that they can not and therefore as said elsewhere, there is a school of thought which argues that the police must be bifurcated into (1) crime investigation and (2) law and order. The bifurcation can only ensure justice to people so that each wing do everything in a professional way. Today, everyone is a jack of all trades and such a policy helps only to administer wounded justice to people.

What was "justice"? Nobody taught the concept to Indian police in the British Raj. Laws were enacted and punishments were prescribed. A repressive police force was created and they were allowed to administer justice and as functionaries who did not know what was justice started administering justice in a crude way. Periodically, the strength of police was increased. Service was not at all a concern of the police and the police meant only repression and suppression of the Indian masses. In 1908, Lord Morley, Secretary of State in a private letter wrote to the Viceroy: "I must confess to you that I am watching with the deepest concern and dismay the thundering sentences that are now being passed for sedition etc....I can not on any terms whatever consent to solicit to defend such monstrous things. I do therefore urgently solicit your attention to these wrongs and follies. We must keep order, but excess of severity is not the path to order. On the country, it is the path to the bomb". If the Secretary of State thought thus, it meant more than what could be read from his letter to the Viceroy. In simplest words, one could see a sort of jungle law administration and the police was a means for that.

The philosophies which guided the British in administration of justice in Great Britain were not of any much relevance in India, for, the British thought that the police for Indians as repeatedly said earlier was just a repressive force and nothing more. The British and other European philosophers have been talking a lot about ethics in administration and what was the *police ethics*? The British have been talking a lot about *Magna Carta* and how did they respect the contents in *Magna Carta* as far as the Indian police and policing the Country might have been concerned? L.F. Rushbrook Willians, a professor in Allahabad said in 1922-23: "Public opinion therefore tends to look upon the constable as a symbol of oppression and restraint...." To quote him more: "The policeman, it must regretfully be stated has a bad name in India; he is accused both of tyranny and of corruption...a force which is still largely illiterate, none-too-well paid and wholly unstimulated by healthy police opinion...." Until the police of India, like the police of England, enjoy the whole-hearted support of the average citizen....India can never possess the kind of force she needs".

How could the British police achieve the whole-hearted support of the people in Great Britain? How could not the police in the British Raj in India achieve the same from the people of India? The reasons were obvious and the British knew them. But, they did not want a police system which was people - friendly and justice oriented. The British who were concerned more with their economic imperialism and with their ethnic superiority than with administration of justice could, of course, make use of the police for their advantage. Anything alone for their advantage was right for them and certainly their methods of administering justice could only cause rebellion and wide-spread disharmony in the Country. India rebelled against the British and the rebellion produced further problems for the police. The basic values of human personality as the British conceived them for their people in London - man's integrity, his freedom, his worth as a human person - were subjected to cruel restraints for the Indian masses and the police were misused as effective weapons for the same. When India became independent, could the Indian administrators solve the problems? They did not and of course, the history had influence on them. The Indian administrators faced an existential crisis - a crisis that concerned the very nature and meaning of police works, duties and responsibilities. To begin with, the police in democratic India did not have a philosophy of life. They continued to live in the imperialist philosophy and they resorted to repressive methods. The police in Indian democracy could not and did not think that they were people's police. Without a proper development of a work-culture in which the concerns and worth of every individual find meaningful expression, the police in any democracy can not hope to deal successfully with the dissatisfactions that disturb deeply today. The police needed a philosophy - a philosophy of outlook and a philosophy of work-culture. Whether or not the police in India have a philosophy today may be a matter of dispute. In any case, there is an attempt to develop a philosophy for the police now. There are indications that a new philosophy for the police is in fact taking shape now and for the next millennium. The passing of the Protection of Human Rights Act - 1993 and the establishment of Human Rights Commissions in the Country do take the police to a new direction. The National Police Commission: 1977-81 made many suggestions, but they were not implemented. Today, the suggestions have become obsolete and any suggestion which were made without recognizing human rights could not and can not survive any longer in the new millennium. There must develop a natural relationship with the police. Democracy is taken to be the desirable political ideal in India - a democracy in which each individual is accepted as he is - where each person is well recognized as a person with human dignity. In such a liberal democracy, the philosophy must be human rights friendly and in such a democracy, administration of wounded justice has little or no scope.

5

Wounded Justice:

The Police Instincts and the People's Expectations

What is the philosophy of police today? Many do not know it. Then what was police philosophy during the British rule? Many do not know that too. Then how can we decide the difference between the two? I asked once in my class consisting of police officers to tell me the difference between the police today and the police in the British past. Many tried to answer the question in their own ways, but one of them said: "Today the police are people centered whereas they were Government centered during the colonial past". Man at the centre of police action is, no doubt, a good attitude and if the police are able to divert their concentration from the Government in power to the man in a democracy, then there is little scope for wounded justice administration. The question is: "Is it possible to do so?"

What is the meaning of "man-centered (?)"- or - people centered (?) police administration? An extract from the 1996-97 report of the National Human Rights Commission reads: "With each succeeding year, the conviction of this Commission has increased, that there can be no substantial improvement in the human rights situation in this country unless those whose duty it is to protect such rights, ceases to be predators themselves. This observation is especially relevant to the police, for the Commission has observed that a majority of the complaints that it has received relate to the conduct of the police, many questioning its integrity. In particular, the complaints suggest that police investigators can not be trusted, because of the extraneous pressures, political, executive or otherwise, that are brought to bear on the process".

The report of the National Human Rights Commission points to the lack of police integrity and their susceptibility to pressures. Logically, it follows that the police in such situation can not become people centered. In Calcutta Review published in 1884, one reads: "....the police are usually useless, that is, they are paid by the State for no appreciable services to the community, or else they are a positive evil". If the police lack integrity or are found to be susceptible to external pressures, then the police today become no better than the police in India during 1884. Both police in 1884 and 2000 then do not become people centered or justice oriented. Why?

Bertrand Russel, the English philosopher and reformer once said: "the instinctive part of our character is very malleable. It may be changed by beliefs, by material circumstances, by social circumstances and by institutions". If the police must behave in a people centered way - justice oriented manner, then they must not behave instinctively. Instinct must give way to intelligence and intelligence alone can ensure proper justice. The history of police in India shows that instinctive behaviors were plenty in their activities. Calling epithets, shouting at people in filthy language, uttering vulgar expressions, using third degree methods, asking the detinues to remain in under garments or without any dress in police lockups etc. were expressions of the instinctive character of the police organization in general and of individual police officers in particular. As

Bertrand Russel said, the instinctive characteristics/character could be changed only by beliefs. Somehow or other, a belief has gone into the police that the people who approach them are antisocial elements, criminals, rogues or people of similar nature. No decent woman wills to go to a police station alone as she is afraid of interpretations or attacks. As the police entertain misconceptions about the nature of people who approach them and as the people have some conceptions of police - true or erroneous -, it is likely that they behave instinctively and that behavior can be changed only if there is a change in their beliefs. Psychologists may attest to the view that wounded justice may be resulted from an instinctive behavior or from erroneous concepts/beliefs.

The instinctive character of police can be changed by material circumstances, by social circumstances or by institutions. Were there any change in the material or social circumstances of the policemen in the past and even now? Policemen were always poorly paid employees. For example, the salary of a police constable, as indicated earlier in Bengal police during 1861 was Rs. 6,7 and 8 depending upon the grade each one occupied and the same of the inspector general of police was Rs. 3000 per month. The disparity in the pay of the constable and of the inspector general of police was very wide. Even today, there exists wide disparity between the two. The policemen were considered as unskilled labourers - they were illiterate - were employed for orderly duties and menial works - were treated without respecting their dignity etc. in the past. Have the material and social circumstances changed now so that the policemen at the lower ranks feel self-esteem and dignity? If the situation has not changed, wounded justice will be resulted. Research studies give enough evidence to show that the officers/men accused of having charge-sheeted and punished for custodial death usually come from the lower ranks in police service. What is more? The officers/men at the bottom level of police administration are often blamed for human rights violations. Policemen who are denied of family life and sexual pleasures may be responsible for custodial murder. People who do not respect the policemen have problems with them. They do not respect the policemen because they do not feel like respecting them. They give low social status to the policemen and precisely therefore, they do not obey them. Necessarily, the policemen express their instincts when they interact with people and they may do so by employing torture or by uttering filthy expressions. Necessarily, the instincts are closely connected to wounded justice administration in police work. The psychologists may say that the relationship is cause - effect which means that the instincts cause wounded justice. The instinctual behaviour of police is found to be centuries old behaviour and no conscious attempt had been made to change the instinctual character of the police in India. There is a view that the behaviour of police could be changed through proper training and value inculcation; but the Governments which came into power from time to time in independent India did not care much for improving the training of police or, for remoulding their character. Of course, Government of India appointed a Central Committee under the chairmanship of Prof. Gore in 1971 for improving the training of police, but the implementation of the Committee's recommendations has been frustratingly slow or indifferently executed in many States.

Today, there is a revolution in information technology, Correspondingly, the quality and technology of investigation, management, communication etc. must be improved and upgraded. Criminals are using increasingly sophisticated methodology and are found to harness the latest technology for committing crime. The nature of crimes too has witnessed a shift in the recent past. In the changed scenario, the instinctual behaviour of police, which perhaps was successful once upon a time, may not yield any good output in the years to come.

Training has to be improved and the human resources should be enviably good. Police job, particularly at the bottom level, has not attracted many. It was unattractive because of the hard work, megre pay, job hazards and the low status enjoyed by the constables. In the history of police in India for the last hundred and fifty years, the investigation of crime has not yielded good results in an enviable way in any part of the Country. Just see the crime statistics and it may be seen that the crimes are on the increase. Look at the conviction rate after a trial from the courts of law. It is constantly and continuously on the decrease. Corruption could be seen in police and for example in 1880, two hundred policemen were caught convicted for their corrupt connivance with dacoits. During 1877-78, some policemen in Gaya district, as pointed out earlier were found to have involved in the commission of dacoities, mail robberies etc. Of course, they were dismissed from service. If the paper reports are true, there are many policemen involved in criminal activities now. Also, there are many senior and middle level police functionaries maintaining unholy relations with underworld criminals. During the British rule, the white officers did not have - or were not found to have involved - any unholy *nexus* with unscrupulous people in India. "What does it matter to me" - a senior police officer living amidst many rich and affluent people asked - "If hundred criminals go to jails after a *thorough investigation* of crimes conducted by me if I do not make a fortune from the job I do". He continued: "Make as much fortunes as possible so that one can employ a good lawyer if at all he is caught. On the other hand, if he does not have enough money to defend himself, then he is lost in life". This sort of an attitude was not there among the police functionaries in the British past.

There is no meaning in talking about justice, injustice, miscarriage of justice, wounded justice etc. to such functionaries. Justice, as pointed out elsewhere is the '*Maat*' and it means goodness, truth and righteousness. In administering justice to anyone, if one sees a blackspot in goodness, truth and righteousness, then I may call it to be wounded justice. Wounded justice needs not be injustice or miscarriage of justice. It is a wound in justice and that is all about it.

Police is to administer justice or aid the administration of justice. If people entrusted with such noble duties become corrupt, then where do the people go for getting justice? Do the people have a right to demand justice from police? In the colonial past, the people did not have, but in the democratic present the people do have. Experience so far proves that there are many influences, introductions and '*isms* working in police so much so that people resort to many means to get justice. Stirner once expressed the idea when he said that "a handful of might is better than a bagful of right". Yet, this is true and that is what the politicians say when they speak about justice from police. A police officer once told me that he is literally afraid of the so called "weaker sections" of the society. He said that the women members of the suppressed/oppressed class, labourers, students and so on come to police and they dictate terms. If they are not listened to and later acted upon as the police think proper they blame the police telling that they are ill-fated to suffer the miscarriage of justice - or - wounded justice from police just because they belong to the handicapped sections of the society. This, of course, is an approach which people adopt to make the police to administer *justice* in the way they want to. Nietzsche said long ago: "Verily I laughed many a time over the weaklings who thought themselves good because they had lame paws". To this I may also add what Pericles uttered: "You know as well as we do that right, as the world goes, is only in question for equals in power; the strong do what they can and the weak suffer what they must". All throughout the history of justice administration one notices this fact. Socretus too said: "Listen then. I proclaim that might is right, and justice is the interest of the stronger....Now, when a man has taken away the money of the citizens and made slaves of them, then instead of swindler and thief he is called happy and blessed by all. For injustice is censured because those who censure it are afraid of suffering and not from any scruple they might of doing injustice themselves".

When the police system fails to perform its duties and responsibilities, the society devises and designs its own system to protect its interest. The police report of 1883 mentions about a system of village protection in Hoshangabad. According to the system, all able bodied men collect at a particular place and when an alarm is sounded informing the approach of the dacoits, they combine together with all available arms for the defence of the village. If this was so in the past, the same situation continues even today. The people make their own security arrangements instead of depending upon the police service. Security service has been institutionalized now. People employ private detective agencies to collect evidence in criminal and civil cases. People including private financiers and banks employ *goondas* and other able bodied men to realize their loans. Politicians, organized crime syndicates, Mafia criminals make their own arrangements to protect their interest. The developing gang culture administers justice in their own way. They do not depend upon the police. The underworld criminals have developed their own administration of justice. The politician - bureaucrat - businessmen nexus functions with their special code of conduct. Criminal cases in large numbers are acquitted and the people increasingly understand the futility of criminal investigation. It has now become an item of news in the media whenever a court convicts an offender. The press reports the news in such a way that the readers get an idea that something impossible has taken place. The press publishes the photographs of the investigating officers, prosecuting counsels and the convicting judges! While on one side, it declares to the people that the justice system works and on the other side, it again makes clear that conviction in criminal cases is a rare occurrence which captures media attention and acquires news values.

Unpopularity of Police and Wounded Justice

Has police been ever popular with the people of India? Today, attempts are made to make "popular police service", "people's police service" and to finally to inculcate the idea that "the people are the police and the police are the people". Whatever that be, politicians read in between the lines and beyond the lines. They start attaching political colouring to the proposed schemes to make the police popular. The politicians' apprehensions may not be always without any basis. Even an impartial man may say that the intentions of the Government in introducing "people's police" scheme is at best suspicious.

"Police are for all, but belong to none"—this is my view. Nobody wants to own the police and precisely therefore they become unpopular. During the latter part of the 19th century, the Commissioner of Police, Lucknow, wrote: "the police are a disreputable body, and they know it; they are, therefore, mistrusted and hampered even when they wish to work openly and fairly". The senior commissioner in the province further said: "Every year convinces me that....the police are honeycombed with corruption. Facts constantly come to my knowledge which convince me of this, although it would be hard to prove them in a judicial inquiry". What do these opinions mean? It means only one thing - i.e., if the police do justice, they become popular with the people. On the other hand, if they do injustice, they become popular only with the vested interests.

Has the situation improved now? The police, even when one hundred years have elapsed since the Commissioner and senior commissioner, Lucknow made their opinion, continues to be disreputable, Why? The reason may be found in the morality of the policeman. The "ethical man" in every policeman/officer must accept his moral obligations, whenever he administers justice in society. A 'legal man' is seen in every policeman and the 'legal man' must administer justice to people in society. Instead, whenever a policeman does something being guided by the pleasures he derives when he does something, he becomes unpopular. Every policeman's life has a direction and purpose and he can not ignore them. He must become the master of himself. Instincts do not have and should not have any place when he enforces law or administers justice. Whenever a suspect is interrogated, evidence must speak and not the instinct of the interrogator. Whenever, a raid is conducted, emotions must be controlled and the sense of justice must prevail. A policeman is free to act, but his freedom must be exercised legally, morally and intelligently. Whenever a policeman behaves thus, he achieves genuine selfhood and self-esteem. Soren Kierkegaard, an existential philosopher says that every man must create for himself the moral values that enables him to 'exist as a man'. Every policeman must exist as a man - as a legal man - as a moral man and for that he must or he can create his own morality basing on goodness, truth and righteousness - the *Maat*. In such a situation there may not be any scope for injustice or wounded justice. This was not seen in policemen in the past. It is not seen even in the present and that is the precise reason why he becomes unpopular with the people. In police life, a policeman may encounter situations where it is simply impossible to follow the legal imperative of duty. A legal minded policeman then feels desperate, for he is unable to do what he knows he ought to do. He wants to arrest a culprit, but he can not because the culprit is a person who is very influential. He is then faced with an impossible legal dilemma. Not to arrest the culprit, he knows, is a wrong or is a wounded justice administration. He experiences guilt; yet he tolerates the wounded justice.

The British, in the Indian Police Act-1861, under section 23 said: "It shall be the duty of every police officer promptly to obey and execute all orders and warrants *lawfully* issued to him by any competent authority....". Though the law put "lawfully issued" in the section, no police officer/man had any discretion to examine the lawfulness of the order issued to him by an authority. As a result he had no option but to execute all orders irrespective of their lawfulness and unlawfulness. There have been situations in which the policeman on duty experienced a sense of guilt when he obeyed the orders. In one such case, a policeman made a clean confession of his guilt feelings after several years of his executing an unlawful order. It was a case in which a Naxilite was shot dead in a fake encounter. The National Police Commission takes cogniscence of such fake encounters in recent times. A legally committed policeman-especially when he has an upright conscience and moral sense–may experience anguish, fear and trembling when he involves himself in the commission of wounded justice administration. Throughout the history of police in India from 1861 till date, one may find torture in police stations or in police custody. Several commissions have been appointed from time to time to probe into individual cases of torture in police custody. Amnesty international, recently, said that torture has been institutionalized in Indian police.

Jean-Paul Sartre, a humanistic existentialist, once said: "Man as such is nothing. He will become only what he makes of himself....man creates himself, his own nature, by acting on the world outside and beyond him. The world changes him as it changes and he changes as he changes the world. Man as such, then, never is but is always becoming". Taking Sartre's view, can we say that - (1) a policeman as such is nothing, (2) he will become only what he makes of himself. Yes, it is one hundred per cent true as far as a policeman is concerned. If a policeman wants to be justice friendly, then he can and that too only what he makes of himself. In British India, there is evidence to show that the police registered false cases and effected unjust arrests of innocent people. They concocted evidence and saw that they were punished. Research studies now conducted too bring out the same story of torture and concoction of evidence. Admitting that such indecent acts by police is a gross administration of wounded justice, one may further add that a policeman makes only what the wants to make of himself. If he wants to be justice friendly, he can be; otherwise not.

"I am what I have" - said Jean Paul Sartre. My merit, my recognition, my acceptance, my unique position in the department, my authority, my power, my men and thus the policeman has many "HAVES" which ordinary people in society too have. Whatever that be, any police officer who wants to get quick results by short cut methods, by employment of third degree methods etc. may achieve success, but the intensity of wounded justice administration in such cases may be very severe. "I am what I have" and thus "the police are what the police have" and the history of police from 1861 makes the police what they are today.

The British did not import a police system to India, they rather created one. A police system was essential for them. They were not concerned about the expectations of the people, rather were caring about the protection of their self interest in India. In their existential philosophy, they were not at all concerned with the *essence* of police and their *services* to India and Indians. The police were given powers to retain the British rule in India. More often than not, the police behaved from their instinctual ego, and not from their intellectual ego. The police in India were dynamic, but only to maintain the British interest. They were not good investigators, for investigation of crime was not an item of importance or priority for the British. The Indian policemen were taken to the parade ground and they were given almost an army like training. They called the police "FORCE" and they never wanted the police to be a "SERVICE" to the people of India. The result was the formation of brutal police force. When India became independent, the same culture continued and is still continuing without much changes in police attitude and approaches. The police did everything to retain the British in power during their reign and they do many things now to maintain the ruling political party in power now. Every policeman thus becomes a faceless member of the force/service as the case may be. He reconciles with his fate and claims that things can not be other than what they are. An awareness of a policeman's social responsibility, his responsibility to protect the human rights of others and his responsibility to avoid wounded justice administration etc, are topics which are now included in the syllabus for the training of policemen/officers. This was not done earlier.

What is the essence of police service? The essence consists in administering fair and just justice. Any existence of a police service without the real essence for it is meaningless. Police must exist with an essence. Philosophers said that the essence of man is more important than his existence. The existentialist philosophers argued that the existence of man is more important than his essence. Let the philosophers argue one another, but I for one think that the essence and existence, both are equally important. One can not exist without the other. As far as the police are concerned, I feel, both the essence and existence are important. The British created a police service and the service had existence, but no essence. As the essence was lacking in Indian police, the police behaved in the way they wanted. They behaved instinctively. While the British was interested in the existence of a brutal police force in India, they were very keen to have a police service with true essence in London. Thus, one sees two kinds of policemen in India and in Great Britain. Police for the Englishman is a Bobbey whereas the police in India is not.

After India became independent, the political parties which formed the governments were also interested in the existence of a police force for them. They too did not take account of the "essence" of police service in democratic India. The tragedy has been that the police *exists* without proper *essence* and this is one of the main reasons for the administration of wounded justice even after 50 years' of freedom in our Country. Should we still maintain the view that police, first of all, exists or must exist as a force? Or should we say that the police, first of all, must have the essence of a service agency? - Or should the police have the existence as a force and the essence as a service? Or should the police have the existence as a service and the essence as a service? In my view, the police in a democracy must have the existence as a service and essence as a service if they want to avoid wounded justice administration at any cost. When the police consider their existence as a service and essence as a service, they are performing their duties and responsibilities, not instinctively but in accordance to public expectations. In such a system, there will be accountability - transparency - and sensitivity. They render their services to the mankind and in such a service, there is no scope for wounded justice administration. For example, think of a police officer who orders to shoot people at sight and when he orders so he knows that he may be sending some people to their death. If he believes that it is his service to humanity he does so, then he administers just-just justice. Police can not do anything without the sanction of law. They have a lot of rules, laws, and regulations before, behind, above, around and below them. If one can exercise the law with a service-mindedness, then he becomes a noble policeman who understands the meaning of his existence and essence in a democracy.

Just go through the report submitted by J. Beames' Committee in 1891which enquired into the causes of failure or defects (i.e., wounded justice administration) which existed in police. The Committee found that careless and indifferent recording of the first information relating to a crime, delay in initiating investigation, perfunctory methods of investigation, failure or refusal to send evidence and undue reliance given to oral evidence and confessions etc. as the main imperfections in police work and they affected adversely the trials of the cases. Take any study report on the defects in the existing police system. One may notice the same thing which Beames' Committee said in 1891 being repeated in 2000. I studied the issue in detail and my observations were published as books. I could see the same things in a stronger way working today. Just look at the reports of the Police Commissions appointed by various States from time to time and also the reports of the National Police Commission. They too repeat the same thing in an elaborate way. So, what is wrong with the system? Undesirable things that existed in the colonial rule continue to be existing in a Country which became free in 1947. Why? The primary reason is that there was no shift in police philosophy given till today. The existence of police is given more priority than its essence. Now it is high time that we think of giving existence and essence of police service an equal importance in administration of justice.

Why did the British recruit illiterate people to police service? Was it because they did not get sufficient number of literate people to work as constables? If that was the case, why are they not provided with facilities to study while they were in service? Why did the British fix Rs. 5 or Rs. 6 or Rs. 7 etc. as the monthly salary of the constables? Did they really want to avoid educated and intelligent people joining the police? Anyway, the Beames' Committee made a suggestion for improving the quality of crime-work by police. The Committee recommended to make a distinction between the literate and the illiterate branches of the police. The literate branch consisted of inspectors, sub-inspectors and probationers to be employed on reporting and detection of crime and usually on work requiring mental training and intelligence. The illiterate branch consisted of head constables and constables to be employed on guard, escort, town duty and all works requiring knowledge of drill and discipline. The intentions of the British in recruiting the illiterate with a petty pay as constables need no further explanations. They wanted *animal-men* and they succeeded in it. These *animal-men* would do many things as caused by their instincts. My concern is about those who were recruited to police service after India became independent. Even then, educational qualifications were of no much importance for enlistment to police service as constables. Even today, one sees semi-literate constables, head constables and assistant sub-inspectors in police! What good can come from such people? It shows that a police system which gave undue importance to the existence and no importance to the essence of the service continued to work even after India became independent. Wounded justice, then, becomes an inevitable outcome. Even today, the scriptory works in police stations and almost all works connected with crime investigation are done by ill-qualified or underqualified or unqualified head constables. There is research evidence to show that the investigation in many cases are far away from being satisfactory and criminal cases in large numbers end in acquittals. As said earlier, there is a suggestion now to bifurcate the police into two separate branches - i.e., (1) Crime Investigation and (2) Law and Order. However the proposal remains as a proposal which shows that the administration still refuses to accept the essence of police work. They do not want to end the wounded justice administration and do not want to live up to the expectations of the people with whose money the service is maintained. To be more open, crime investigation receives only low priority today as the Governments and the police administration are still concerned more with law and order management than crime investigation. If the case is not sensational, the administration is not serious in investigating it properly. As a result, the people who have expectations lose their trust on police investigation. Very often, they demand investigation by the CBI even in less serious cases. Even the

CBI becomes targets of negative comments, criticism and appreciation for the investigative works they do from the courts, people and the press. How long can this continue? How long can the people tolerate wounded justice administration? They become topic of discussion in many fora in these days. As Plato told to Hermias: "every one must cooperate in the great work of reforming mankind according to the principles of justice", we may hope that the politicians, administrators, press and the people will cooperate to wipe off wounded justice administration if they want to ensure justice to mankind.

6

Wounded Justice:

An Age-Old Evil and Public Reaction

Homo homini lupus (man is a wolf to man) - said Schopenhauer. Robert Ardrey considers human aggression as the manifestation of an innate drive that man inherits from his killer-ape ancestors. Torture in police custody is an age old evil in Indian police. Forget about the Torture Commission Report of 1855. Torture is a recurring phenomenon. Aggression and torture in police continued unceasingly and whenever they occurred, the people expressed their protests against them. Torture and torturing a suspect in police custody may seem for some police officers/men at first a triumph. But in reality, this is not correct. The story of Indian police points to that reality. Torture has brought only bad name to police and at times, employment of torture is justified by the public. The committee appointed under Mr. W. Kaye in June 1890 to inquire into, inter alia, the existing methods of police investigation wrote:

"The intensely bitter feeling with which the bulk of the force appears to be regarded by the public has come to us, we are fain to confess, as a surprise....One of the first points that struck us in conducting this inquiry was the intense dread which the police as a body inspired....Another feature of the evidence, and one on which we cannot too strongly insist, is the fact that service in the police is just as unpopular, and just as much shunned, as are the police officials themselves". The Committee accused the police of oppression, tyranny, corruption, abuse of power, misuse of authority, employment of torture, corruption, concoction and fabrication. The Committee found fault with the material on which the force was created or the system which permitted all these obnoxious practices. The report of the Committee showed lack of character among the police functionaries at that time.

Torture in police stations becomes an incurable disease and one reads it in the first pages of the Torture Commission Report - 1855 and in the front page of this morning's newspaper. The Indian Police Commission: 1902-03 condemns it and the National Police Commission: 1977-81 further condemns it. Several policemen/officers have been punished for it. Researchers have made many suggestions to prevent it. Human Rights activists vehemently oppose it and the United Nations have brought out a Convention Against Torture and Other Degrading Treatment and Punishment. National Human Rights Commission awards compensation to the victims of torture. Yet, torture continues and the evil persists in justice administration for a long time. Justice becomes wounded when torture comes to the scene. Man becomes a beast when he resorts to aggressiveness and torture of people who are defenseless and helpless. John Stuart Mill (1806-1873) said: "No human creatures would consent to be changed into any of the lower animals, for a promise of the fullest allowance of a beast's pleasure, no intelligent human being would consent to be a fool, no instructed person would be an ignoramus, no person of feeling and conscience would be selfish and base, even though they would be persuaded that the fool, the dunce, or the rascal is better satisfied with his lot than they are with theirs".

Training of Police Personnel and Administration of Wounded Justice

No civilized country would tolerate crime investigation by illiterate, ill-informed, unqualified people. There were severe criticisms against police investigation of crimes. Torture and third degree methods were the principal techniques employed by the police to investigate crimes. The investigating officers could not be blamed for what they did, for they knew nothing about scientific and psychological methods of investigating suspects. A training school was started at Bhagalpur for the training of the directly recruited investigating officers in 1895. Another Police Training School was earlier established at Phillaur in Punjab for the training of sub-inspectors in 1892. What type of training was given to them? They were taught something of law, procedure and evidence and were subjected to very severe outdoor training which included even bayonet training. Science and scientific investigation of crime were unknown to them and the result had been continuation or perpetuation of torture and third degree methods of investigation by police.

Lord Curzon in 1902 said: "A Government that gives good laws or good education, or the wherewithal to live, but that places the preservation of internal order and the detection, prevention and punishment of crime in soiled or incompetent hands can not escape severe reproach". He therefore decided to set up a strong Commission to go into every aspect of police administration. Indian Police Commission: 1902-03 was subsequently appointed.

The age-old evil, namely the torture and third degree methods of interrogation, still prevails in Indian Police. National Human Rights Commission, in their annual report 1996-97, has urged to make use of scientific and psychological methods of interrogation. For, the Commission found that the crude methods of interrogation have always caused human rights violations.

XXXIII All India Police Science Congress held in Jammu, during 1999 insisted the necessity of making police interrogation scientific and psychological. It is easier said than done!

Though the British established police training centres to train police investigators of crime, they did not or could not teach their trainees scientific methods of investigation and psychological methods of interrogation. They could not be blamed for it, because the science of investigation and the psychology of interrogation were not developed then. There was no literature or forensic science laboratories were not available then. At the same time, the police were pressured to investigate criminal cases and interrogate suspects in crime. Having little or no knowledge in scientific investigation and psychological interrogation, the ignorant police investigators lavishly resorted to their muscle power. Torture and third degree methods thus became an oft-resorted easy cuts to detect crimes and criminals. No one dared to question the police, for that had further evil consequences. Reiterating what the Commission wrote in 1902: "The police officer, owing to want of detective ability or to indolence, directs his efforts to procure confessions by improper inducement, by threats and by moral pressure.... Sometimes suspects, whom the police officer does not desire to report as under arrest, are kept for days together under so-called 'surveillance', which is nothing else than unauthorized confinement or restraint, a system which affords serious opportunity for malpractices. All this is done to secure evidence in support of the view which the police officer from time to time holds regarding the case. If in his opinion, enough of evidence is not thus obtained to secure a conviction, he will not hesitate to bolster up his case with false evidence. Sometimes, this leads to an innocent person being prosecuted through police mistakes. More often perhaps it leads to guilty persons escaping through the suspicion thrown on the police evidence. Many a good case has been ruined in this way; but the police officer is unduly impelled by the statistical test to try to make his investigation end in conviction. When an investigation fails, the complainant is sometime finally bullied or threatened into acknowledging that a mistake has been made, and that the case is 'false'. When it is successful, the accused is often subjected to unnecessary annoyance; the law about bail is overlooked; the rule limiting the use of handcuffs are forgotten; and no serious effort is made to treat the accused with that consideration as to his food and comfort to which...he is entitled until he is convicted".

What we read above is not taken from a fairy tale or a detective novel. It is the way justice - better, wounded justice, crude justice, injustice, brute injustice - has been administered in this Country of huge population by people who upheld the theories in Magna Carta and other human rights principles. There is no meaning now in blaming anybody and precisely therefore we have to confine ourselves to what is happening here and now. Has the situation changed after a century since the Indian Police Commission: 1902-03 wrote the way as we read above? The condition continues to remain in the same way in most parts of the Country? - in many parts of the Country? - in some parts of the Country? Some critics may say that the conditions have gone worse in democratic India?

If paper reports are true, then there is illegal detention, informal arrests, unauthorized ways of interrogating suspects. When the annual reports of the National Human Rights Commission are read, one takes note of custodial rape, custodial torture/death, killing in fake encounters, stripping in police lock ups etc. If we read the reports of inquiry commissions appointed in all States, we may come across a lot of human rights violations by police. Above all, the verdicts of the higher judiciary make matters clear. Disciplinary inquiries ordered against the delinquents, often, prove that the officers/men are guilty. There are any number of research studies to show that the police make use of cruel, inhuman and degrading methods during the investigation of crimes. It means that the evil persists...wounded justice administration continues in spite of 50 years of democratic rule. Why?

I have made extensive studies about the causes of miscarriage of justice and my findings have been published in four volumes. I do not want to repeat my research observations already brought out earlier. Wounded justice administration via age old evils continues even today because of several factors. More than anything, the police officers must be mentally prepared to accept that the evils exist and the evil is evil if at all vested interests sugarcoat it. No evil can be good or made good by making it to appear that the evil is a necessary evil. For, some policemen/officers firmly think that torture, concoction of evidence, human rights violations etc. become sometimes necessary evils with some category of people. Whatever may be their arguments, it becomes necessary to tell them what is right and what is wrong in police work - what is just and what is not just in administration of justice. Lack of conviction about the need to become just in police administration seems to be root cause of all problems connected with wounded justice administration.

Concepts of Right and Wrong

Police in India, today, unquestionably accept their own practices and standards as right. They ignore or condemn those views and opinions, practices and standards which differ from their own. Torture of suspects, concoction of evidence, illegal detention, informal arrests etc. which are seen today are centuries old practices and standards in police sub-culture. Precisely therefore, they can not reject them all on a sudden, one day very soon. For example, the human rights laws came into existence when the Protection of Human Rights Act - 1993 was enacted. All on a sudden, the police were compelled to avoid their hitherto followed practices and standards. Necessarily, it caused tension in them. When India became independent, the police were allowed to continue their old standards and practices. As a result, they thought that they were right in what they have been doing. In my early days as a boy, I honestly thought that the police had the power and authority to employ torture on people. For, I had not, till then, seen a torture free police service. Hence I thought that the police were right in what they were doing. Now I know that I was wrong, but I know that many policemen/officers find it extremely difficult to accept the new standard. 'What a police without the authority to threaten people, and torture them if necessary'– this seems to be the approach of the policemen/officers.

Protagoras (481-411 B.C.) a Sophist philosopher said that all moral standards are relative. I think that some policemen/ officers still hold the view of Protagoras. They say that what is right for the police may not be right for others. Torture is good for detecting crimes especially from property offenders and it needs not be right for a human right activist. What is good for the police is good because it works well with criminals. Torture, they say, may not be legal in police work, but it becomes, sometimes, necessary and in such situations when it becomes a necessary evil, then it is legal as well. This sort of approach I may call legal relativism. In such a situation, the policeman becomes the measure of all things. In such a context, the laws governing police work and the policeman cease to have any validity. Therefore, it becomes necessary to educate the policemen about the wrong nature of their arguments and beliefs.

There are laws, rules and regulations. The policemen have to follow them. They can not become their own laws. If the law is that the police shall not employ torture, degrading and cruel treatment to the suspects in their custody, then they have to follow the law, no matter the suspects is a property offender, rapist or murderer. As the policemen are brought up in a culture which accepted torture - in spite of the laws against it -, their thoughts were shaped by that culture. Now the international community says that the police culture in India has been a perverted culture, then their views must be accepted in fairness. As few policemen/officers in the past did accept that the sub-culture in Indian police was not conducive for administration of fair justice. More and more policemen/officers now subscribe to this view. Courts of law, legislators and people endorse the view. The Protection of Human Rights Act-1993 strengthens the movement. Therefore let every policeman cooperate with the movement to avoid administration of wounded justice in India.

Socrates believed that there is a valid standard of right and wrong, of good and evil and that the knowledge of what is right and good is achievable. I have heard such principles of Socrates being taught to police officers by senior ecolones in police, but, most surprisingly they, later follow their *legal relativism* when they face real situations. In other words, they too are not convinced of what they preach and teach. Human rights laws are standards to which all men - the international community - agree or can be led to agree. If the practices and standards followed till now do not have any rational basis or legal sanctity, then they must be avoided whatever may be their practical utility in police work. In spite of all types of tortures, inhuman and degrading treatments that have been resorted to by police from 1861 or earlier in India, the conviction rate in criminal cases has been going down. Why? It shows that the obnoxious and people unfriendly approaches had no practical utility or long term relevance. There must be the professional integrity and intellectual honesty when the policemen/officers adhere to certain principles, arguments, practices and standards. From my long association with police, what I understand is that the police are not intellectually prepared to accept the human rights principles now as they feel that they will then be handicapped or chained to do things as they like. It is therefore necessary that we must prepare the police to prepare an intellectual land to accept the human rights principles.

Jeremy Bentham (1748-1832), an English philosopher had some influence on the British. It is believed that his doctrine of free will and hedonism has influenced the British even in the drafting of the Indian Penal Code. The greatest happiness principle which was later called *utilitarianism* by John Stuart Mill did influence the British administrators even in making policies for Indian police. The British policy in India was *utilitarian* and they used the police for it. Anything that produced "benefit, advantage, pleasure, good or happiness or to prevent the happening of mischief, pain, evil or unhappiness, to the party whose interest is considered" was utility for Bentham and for the British police in India. Although the British appointed Police Commissions and Committees for improving the police work, they were not keen in executing the recommendations of the Commission/Committees unless they were beneficial for them. Anything that was beneficial for the British was right for them. Use of torture, employment of third degree methods, treating the suspects in a cruel or degrading way etc. were not of great importance for the British. The supervisory ranks in police-and mostly they were British officers-took no special interest to stop such degrading, coercive, humiliating treatment of Indians in Indian police stations. Their permissiveness allowed a sub-culture to develop in police and that sub-culture continued to dominate the police administration even after India became independent. Still, one may say that the same sub-culture prevails in police stations in certain parts of the Country. Therefore what is required now is to create a change in police attitude and make them accept human rights friendly attitude in police work.

They must accept what is right and wrong in police work as Zen Buddhism says:

"If you want to get the plain truth,
Be not concerned with right and wrong,
The conflict between right and wrong
Is the sickness of the mind"

The police have some accepted standards, practices, sub-cultural norms etc. They have a lot of laws, rules and regulations to follow. They have the power and authority. They have the discretion and freedom. They can properly use them. They can also misuse or abuse them. A police officer/man who suffers from the sickness of mind always administers wounded justice.

Science and Psychological Approach

Psychology of interrogation is a special branch in police science/studies. Nevertheless, the branch is Greek to many police officers. A vast majority of police functionaries from the director general of police to the constable are not qualified in social sciences such as criminology, psychology, sociology etc. and therefore they do not possess any special knowledge in interrogation psychology. I am told that the subjects called police interrogation/police interviewing are not seriously taught to the officers of the Indian police service! And, certainly they are not subjects that can be taught by a few lectures during the induction course. As a result, police investigators usually lack interrogation skills, interviewing techniques and this deficiency in them is covered or compensated through torture, coercion, or use of third degree methods. I do not think that any police training institution in India takes the issue seriously. In such a deplorable situation, necessarily wounded justice may be seen.

Science and scientific investigation had no place in crime investigation during the British Raj. Indian Evidence Act - 1872 gave a lot of importance to the oral testimony of witnesses. Scientific evidence was considered only as an opinion evidence and it was rejected by courts whenever there was oral evidence.

The investigators of the British police had little or no knowledge in scientific investigation or if at all they had some knowledge in the application of science for the cause of investigation, there were no forensic science laboratories and forensic scientists to extend help to the investigators. An extract from the report of the Indian Police Commission: 1902-03 is worth quoting or needs to be quoted once again to show how the British police investigated crimes. "The police officer may levy a fee or receive a present for every duty he performs. The complainant has often to pay a fee for having his complaint recorded. He has to give the investigating officer a present to secure his prompt and earnest attention to the case. More money is extorted as the investigation proceeds....People are harassed...sometimes by having to accompany him from place to place, sometimes by attendance at the police stations....sometimes by threats of evil consequences to themselves or their friends (especially to the women of the family) if they do not fall in with his view of the case, sometimes by invasion of their houses by low caste people on the plea of searching for property....From all this deliverance is often to be brought only by payment of fees or presents in cash. The station house officer will sometimes hush up a case on payment of his terms; he will receive presents from parties and their witnesses; he will levy illicit fees from shopkeepers and others for service rendered; or to obviate vexatious espionage...." and thus goes the narration. What sort of justice was it? People still speak of the *British sense of justice* and I do not know what do they mean by such phrases and comments.

The sub-culture that existed during the colonial police administration was transferred to India even when she became independent. The inherited vices and injustices continued to rule the police work under the Indian masters. People thus became the victims of wounded justice administration even under Indian rule. The Indian police in the democracy further conditioned the people to tolerate everything police did in the name of justice administration or in the pretext of justice administration. What is more? The police officers search the houses of the suspects in crime over and over again during night hours–always disturbing the members of the family and offering mental shocks. They forcefully take the suspects, his family members and used to commit many atrocities. Research studies show that corruption and corrupt practices are seen in every police work just like they were noticed by the Indian Police Commission: 1902-03. Political interference is seen always and even today, stories of harassment, humiliation, torture, informal arrest, illegal detention, human rights violations, registration of false cases, concoction of evidence, production of tutored witnesses, manipulation of facts, suggestion of falsehood, suppression of truth, perfunctory investigation, sweet heat contracts with the accused, partsian treatment etc. etc. are heard. In such a situation, people have their own apprehensions about the administration of justice. Justice becomes wounded when it is not administered justly.

Moral Collapse and Legal Relativism

The British destroyed the police morality in India and the Indian administrators permitted the police to follow the sub-culture transmitted by the British. The result has been wounded justice administration. How can we escape the dangers of the wounded justice administration? We must build a justice system which is just for all - everywhere. For this, the police must derive their moral and legal principles entirely from the categorical imperatives of their duty - from the essence of police service. Emmanuel Kant says: "Always act on that maximum which can at the same time be made a universal law of conduct". Can this be possible in police work? He continues: "In order to find out whether our conduct is actually right, right for everyone, we must universalize our principles of behaviour". For example, a police officer keeps a suspect for several days in his custody and what legal justification has he got to do so? He must ask a question to himself: "What would happen to justice administration if every police officer does the way I am doing– and that too with all suspects in police custody?" The answer to the question will help him to say whether or not his conduct conforms to a universal law - whether or not he administers just justice. *Legal relativism* is a dangerous approach and only those who have a moral collapse may resort to *legal relativism*.

Immanuel Kant furthers says: "Act in such a way that you always treat humanity, whether in your own person or in the person of another, never simply as a means but always at the same time as an end". What a noble principle for the police to follow if they want to avoid wounded justice administration! A police officer serves the people and the people are the end in rendering his service. Whenever a police investigator employs torture to elicit information from a suspect, he treats him just as a means to an end, the end being a conviction in the case. On the other hand, whenever a police officer treats his suspects as an end, then he will not and can not use third degree methods on him. For, conviction is not an end in itself, but is a means to an end-the end being correction and reformation of the crime-doer. Seeing the policemen employing torture on a suspect, a morally and legally sane police investigator said: "Please stop. I have to produce him before the Magistrate tomorrow. I can not take his dead body". He said further: "The suspect is the end in justice administration and his correction and reformation is what we want". The British never had this thought whenever they dealt with Indian suspects whereas they had such thoughts whenever they treated their men in England.

Police and Democracy

"Keep away the politicians, we will ensure the finest and fairest justice to men" - said a police officer in a seminar.

Immediately a participant asked: "How can the police keep away the politician when they cling to them for their advantage?" "That is bad"- said the police officer. In a democracy, the politicians play an important role. Both politicians and the police are important in a democratic set up.

During the British rule, politicians were not there to interfere in police work; yet, did the police ensure the fairest and the finest justice to people? The story of Indian police shows that the police can offer justice to people only if they want to do so. John Dewey says: "Democracy is the best form of Government, not because it is the most efficient....but the people tolerate both stupidity and graft on the part of our public officials". Police administer wounded justice to people, because the people tolerate it. Politicians in a democracy may have a partial interest. The police must have only one interest - i.e., justice, fair justice, total justice and equal justice. If the police do not fulfil their duty according to the people's wish, the politicians come with their partial interest and the arrival of politician to a police officer shows that people have more faith in a politician than in a police officer. Certainly, the police officers will be cautious whenever politicians and mediamen approach them.

Policemen/officers in a democracy are the servants of the people. The people are their patrons. Police station is a public facility in a democracy. Policemen/officers are accountable to the people and precisely therefore there can not exist a police service without the politicians playing their role. Anybody in a democracy may question the police. If wounded justice is administered, the public litigation societies take up the issue with the High Court of Judicature. Politicians conduct jadhas, dharnas and street corner meetings to speak in favour or against the police. Police in a democracy become a topic of discussion among the people. In a democracy, people are free.

The jump from the colonial rule to democratic rule was a *frog-jump*, but the Indians could not fully realize the implications of such a *frog-jump*. That was the reason why the political leadership and the police administration permitted the age old police evils to continue even in democratic India. Mahatma Gandhi once said : "The police that I would maintain would be a body of reformers". Anyway that did not happen in India even after 50 years of democracy. "It should be remembered that the first duty of the police is to obtain the goodwill of the people through their service and their integrity. They occupy a position of great responsibility. They can only discharge their duties well if they have the spirit of service to the country and to the people"- said Pandit Jawaharlal Nehru, the first Prime Minister of Indian Democracy - I do not know what he did for inculcating the values he preached to the policemen! The words like the goodwill of the people, *service* and police *integrity, responsibility, spirit* of service to the country and people etc. are indeed good and inspiring words. But there was no meaningful attempt to translate such high sounding philosophy into the police. It is only in 1971, a Central Committee was appointed to review the training system and still (in 2000), many of the Committee's recommendations remain dormant as they are not meaningfully implemented in many States. In the words of the National Police Commission, I find the implementation of the recommendations of the Central Committee's recommendation was frustratingly slow. I am not interested to elaborate it further in this book. Pandit Jawaharlal Nehru, again, I quote, said: "The special feature of police work is that it has a relation with the public. Police work can be discharged well only when public cooperation is available or when there are good relations between the police and the public. Police work consists of ensuring public safety and security, catching criminals and prosecuting them. These things are possible only when the public are inclined to support the police with love and friendship. If the police have no public support, their work can not be done successfully". O.K., the words of Pandit Jawaharlal Nehru are pregnant with meaning. The police is treated as a service in a democracy, but the idea, it seems, does not go into the actual implementation. Even in the reports of the National Police Commission: 1977-81, the words "police force" are used throughout the pages of he Commission's report. The Commission fails to realize the fact that the repeated use of the concept "police force" gives a perverted view about police functions in a democracy. Even in the questionnaire circulated by the recently appointed Committee on Police Reforms (2000) by Government of India, one notices the word's 'police force' repeatedly used. How unfortunate it is to find such words and concepts used in a questionnaire which is intended to collect data for making a police service for the 21st century? Somehow or other, the idea "police force" still dominates the thinking of those who are to make recommendations to transform a force into a service! Smt. Indira Gandhi, the former Prime Minister of India emphatically said that the "police is not merely a force, but to my mind it is much more a service". It may be added that the police is not "much more a service", but "service" itself. This is the democracy's concept. In the words of I.C.P.R.: "The citizen expects every police officer to have the wisdom of Solomon, the courage of David, the strength of Samson, the patience of Job, the leadership of Moses, the kindness of the good Samaritan, the strategic training of Alexander, the faith of Daniel, the diplomacy of Lincoln, the tolerance of the carpenter of Nazareth and finally, an intimate knowledge of every branch of the natural, biological and social sciences. If he had all these, he might be a good policeman". To this, I add that the policeman can ensure fair justice to the people only if he internalizes these noble thoughts. The story of police shows that no conscious attempts have been made to inculcate those sublime thoughts to the policeman so much so that wounded justice continues to rule the policing in largest democracy in the world. As Jerome Hall puts it: "The policeman who confirms to law is the living embodiment of law, he is its microscam on the level of its most specific incidence. He is literally law in action, for in action law must be specific. He is the concrete distillation of the entire mighty of the historic *Corpus juris,* representing all of it including the Constitution itself".

7

Wounded Justice:

Police Commissions and Politicians

India is a liberal democracy. Sadly enough even after 53 years of independence, the police in India is governed by the archiac Indian Police Act - 1861 and the colonial police culture which is repressive and suppressive in nature. Police commissions were appointed in many States to reorganize the police and that was done mostly after India became independent. The terms of reference to these commissions were almost the same and every commission made many recommendations which were also almost of the same nature. As the political parties which ruled the States were not serious in implementing the recommendations made by the State Level Commissions, their recommendations - most of them - gathered dust as there was no political will to enforce them. There was also no administrative insistence to get them implemented.

Going through the history of Indian police from 1861, one may notice that the British wanted to develop a sense of fear of authority among the Indian population and for that purpose alone they introduced a police system by virtue of the Indian Police Act-1861. Fear of authority was the objective of the British, but respect for the authority is the aim of democracy's police system. In August 1860, as stated elsewhere, the British appointed a Police Commission and they were told to keep in mind that the "functions of a police are either protective and repressive or detective". The Commission prepared a draft of the Police Act. A reading of the Act may convince anybody that the sole purpose of the protective, repressive and detective police force was for the maintenance of the colonial rule in India. There were criticisms and protests against some of the provisions in the Police Act of 1861 as they were capable of being misused by the members of the police force. The story of Indian police after 1861 - after the enactment of the Indian Police Act : 1861 - was the story of the British success in maintaining their domain under a repressive police system.

Lord Curzon in July 1902 appointed a Police Commission. The Commission consisted of five Europeans and two Indians. The terms of reference to the Commission consisted of, *interalia*:

(1) Whether the organization, training, strength and pay of the different ranks of the district police, both superior and subordinate....are adequate to secure the preservation of the public peace and the proper investigation and detection of crime, and, if not, what changes are required in them, respectively, in each province with regard to its local conditions, in order to attain these objects;

(2) Whether existing arrangements secure that crime is fully reported or require to be supplemented in any way; and in particular, whether the village officers and the rural police in each province are efficient aids to the district police in the matter of reporting crime, and, if not, how the relations between the former and the latter can (subject to the condition that the rural police in each province must not be enrolled under the Police Act) be improved

(3) Whether the system of investigating offences now in force in each province, the object being to provide for the full

investigation of all serious crimes, while avoiding interference by the police in trivial matters, is capable of improvement and if so, in what manner; and whether the institution of fully organized Criminal Investigation Departments, either Imperial or Provincial, is recommended"

The terms of reference clearly indicated that Lord Curzon saw the misuse of authority and abuse of power by police from what were happening then since the enactment of the Indian Police Act - 1861. For, the clause about Criminal Investigation Department was incorporated to the terms of reference by Lord Curzon personally. He found that the police then interfered even in trivial matters. No doubt, wounded justice administration was in vogue. The "European Control" over the police and their functions were retained. Records show that the first meeting of the Commission was held at Simla on October 15, 1902 and it was attended only by European members. Again, on the conclusion of their inquiries, the Commission convened a conference of the European inspectors general of police to consider some issues. The Commission observed that the police force in India had utterly failed to secure the confidence and cordial cooperation of the people. How could the police secure the confidence and cordial cooperation of the people when they acted as a repressive and suppressive force? The police had a peculiar philosophy and in such a system, public trust and their willing cooperation were just not possible to get. This is what is seen even today. So long as the police in India functions under the Indian Police Act - 1861, the democracy's police can not command respect from the people. They cannot receive people's cooperation and participation. The Police Commission:

1902-03 realized that the police system which worked under the Indian Police Act-1861 failed miserably even at that time - a century ago. The Indian Police Commission: 1902-03 enumerated the causes of failures and they included among other things, the lack of supervision, insufficient training, corruption, poor pay, and the list was very lengthy. There is no need to write more about what the Indian Police Commission: 1902-03 saw about a hundred years ago. The same reasons were reiterated by the State Police Commissions and even by the National Police Commission when they spoke about police failures. Necessarily, they could not find more causes as they were speaking about a system which worked under the same Police Act - 1861 and the Indian Police Commission: 1902-03 was also doing the same thing.

Wounded Justice and Police Commissions

The Indian Police Commission: 1902-03, while analyzing the causes of police abuses, said: "One is that the investigation of cases has been too far to great an extent entrusted to low paid and unqualified officers....In the police department, where the work is perhaps the most difficult and important in India, Government has been content to have the higher and more responsible officers filled by men deficient in education, intelligence and social status....Everywhere the demand of enlightened opinion is for the reform of the station house officer....?

What do these observations show? They reveal that the Indians were fated to suffer the ill-effects of wounded justice administration for centuries and they had no salvation. No doubt, the sufferings of the Indians under a time worn Police Act and an antiquated police system continue even today and henceforth. Jean-Paul Sartre once said: "It is neither our fault nor our merit if we lived in a time where torture was a daily fact. Chateaubriand, Oradour, the Rue des Saussaies, Dachau, and

Auschwitz have all demonstrated to us that Evil is not an appearance, that knowing its cause does not dispel it, that it is not the effect of passions that might be cured, of an ignorance that might be enlightened that it can in no way be incorporated, into idealistic humanism". Many including all police commissions, several politicians, bureaucrats and police administrators know fully well the different and various causes of wounded justice administration. Nevertheless, knowing the causes can not/does not cure the defect unless they have a political will, executive will and bureaucratic determination to eradicate the same.

As it is observed by many police commissions, the Indian Police Commission: 1902-03 also noticed: "Supervision has been doubtly defective. It has been inefficient as regards ... inspectors, and it has been weak and inadequate as regards the superintendents. As to the inspectors...the public do not regard them as honest...there is incontrovertible evidence to show that success rather than honesty has been qualification for promotions"....

Even today, the same observation is valid. Supervision is defective as many do not know how to supervise. Some hold the view that the superior is always right. They still entertain the feeling that wisdom goes with the superiors. If the superiors are underqualified or educationally weaker than the subordinates, then they see to it that the subordinates accept their '*wisdom*' without questioning. Instances are plenty to show that several criminal cases are lost because of inadequate supervision more than lack of supervision. At the other end, always one may see a suffering victim, a victim who is helpless and defenseless before the powerful supervisor and his *efficient* subordinate. The victims lose all their rights, beginning with their right to talk. The wounded justice administrators want their victims to accept what they do in the name of justice or in the pretext of administering justice. During the British past, an all powered police force tried to force the poor people of this poor country to hold their tongues. They spoke very high of the objectives in the Police Act - 1861, but were mean to administer wounded justice to the illiterate, poor and rustic population in India. After India became independent, very high sounding principles were loudly said and written in the Constitution of the Country. But, as the studies show, they had no relevance at the ground level. C.V. Narasimham, formerly the Director of the Central Bureau of Investigation and Member Secretary, National Police Commission observed: "Police performance, as perceived and experienced by the common people, has not come up to their rising demands and expectations after independence. Increasingly critical of the police, their main charge is that police response to crime situations is mostly conditioned by the predilections and politics of the ruling party and their henchmen down the line, and therefore individual complaints from ordinary people do not receive due attention from the police. The general public tend to see the police, not as an impartial and effective agent of law but as a mere limb of the government that gets influenced and directed by political pressure or the associated bribery and corruption. Such a partisan image of the police, which is an integral part of the criminal justice system, spells ultimate danger to the system itself, if it is allowed to prolong without correction". Narasimham blames the political interference in police work for its maladminstration and wounded justice administration. While accepting the truth containing in his observations, one may say further that the inadequate supervision and lack of supervision by the higher echolones in police service is a serious handicap in administration of fair justice to people. The Indian Police Commission: 1902-03 framed charges against the supervisory ranks. The charges against the superintendents were: "....that they are often not well educated or intelligent men that their training is defective, that their knowledge of the vernacular is not such as to enable them to have free intercourse with the people and to become acquainted with their feelings and circumstances, that they are too much in the hands of their subordinates, that they are not accessible or even courteous to natives, that their views are too narrow and their sense of responsibility too weak to allow them to pay due regard to complaints against their subordinates or strictures on their work or to take due notice of misconduct, that they are too burdened with clerical works and too little helped by qualified assistants to be able to exercise effective supervision and control over the police....The Commission are of opinion that there is a great deal of truth in these complaints".

The same or similar complaints are heard even now about police officers who work at higher levels. The main complaints are that some of them do not know the vernacular, local customs and culture. They live an isolated life as they can not communicate with people. They do not understand the local situations and the feelings of the people. What the Police Commission: 1902-03 observed among the superintendents as early as in the beginning of the last century are seen without an iota of change among some of the superintendents even in the beginning of the present century. The state of affairs does not change - rather had worsened further. They cannot interrogate a suspect, interview a witness, record a statement, understand well the language and many of them are semi-literate in vernacular so much so that they can not exert supervision over their subordinates, rather they are too vulnerable in the hands of their subordinates. The subordinates often laugh at them behind their back and treat them as "no supervisors" in reality. Many subordinates to these superintendents of police are from the same locality, religion, caste, faith, culture and human contacts to which politicians - from local level to State/National level - belong. There exists a politician-police *nexus*. With the help of politicians, the subordinates can easily damage the control system and weaken the normal chain of command that has to work efficiently, if the discipline and health of the system are to be protected. Again to quote C.V. Narasimham, "interference at the operational level in police stations, police circles etc. results in the total by-passing of the supervisory officers in the hierarchy. Subordinate officers see it every day of their official life that their superior officers count little in the ultimate disposal of a matter which lies in the normal course within their official cognizance only. The frequent by-passing of the normal chain of command results in the atrophy of the supervisory culture". How did such a culture develop? The culture developed as a result of the inefficiency of the supervisory ranks either because they were incapable of supervising their subordinates or because they were incapacitated to exercise their supervisory capabilities. Studies show that the former was more responsible than the latter for the weakening of the command structure in police. Whatever may be the causes, the ill-fate is for the citizens of this Country.

Whenever, an efficient, capable and effective subordinate having political *nexus* looks at a superior who is incapable of supervising him, then the superior becomes a *thing* - an *object* - a *body* for him. Annoyed at becoming a *thing* in the hierarchy, the superior may shout at the subordinate who may just ignore him. The superior may accept or reject an idea by looking at the person who proposes it. If it is proposed by someone whom he does not like, he may reject the idea. Even there too, wounded justice administration may be seen. More about the observations made by the Police Commission: 1902-03 and their modern versions as seen in today's police are topics of interest for many.

Police Commission: 1902-03 made remarks about lower level officers as well. The quote: "There are honest and efficient police officers of all grades, though they are represented as being very exceptional in the lower grades....Neither do the Commission forget that much may be said in excuse for the misconduct of the police in the generally indifferent attitude of the people in respect of crime, in the encouragement of corruption by the readiness with which the people offer illegal gratifications, and in the low pay and poor prospects of the police service. But honorable exceptions and mitigating circumstances can not efface the general impression created by evidence recorded. There can be no doubt that the police force throughout the country is in a most unsatisfactory condition, that abuses are common everywhere, that this involves great injury to the people and discredit to the Government, and that radical reforms are urgently required. These reforms will cost much; because the department has hitherto been starved; but they must be effected". The Commission was determined to effect some changes whatever might be the cost involved. For, the Commission was pained to see the sad state of affairs. The Commission had the courage to speak out the truth.

What about the police today? Do they possess the virtues they ought to have in a democracy? A number of films are shown in theatres in these days and the policemen - from the constables upwards to the director general of police - are shown. How? A lot of news comes in the print media and what do the people read about the police and their performance? Is it right to show that the higher level functionaries have unholy relationship with underworld criminals? - with unscrupulous politicians? - with corrupt businessmen? Is it right to show that the policemen at the bottom level are corrupt and unprincipled? People see the movies and it seems that they endorse the views. After reading the news in the press, people make comments: "Incredible, horrible, inhuman, nasty, unimaginable" etc and what do they show? Police and policing a democratic society have special meanings for the people. They have not only legal duties to be performed, but must have social, moral and responsible concerns for the people in society. C.V. Narasimham enumerates a number of typical situations in which the present day police misuse their powers/abuse their authority. They are–

(1) Arrest or non-arrest of a person against whom a case is taken up for investigation by police.

(2) Deliberate handcuffing of a person in police custody merely to humiliate him.

(3) Release or non-release on bail after arrest.

(4) Suppression of material evidence that becomes available during searches by police.

(5) Inclusion or non-inclusion in the charge-sheet placed in court on conclusion of investigation.

(6) Posting or non-posting of police force in an area of apprehended trouble to create an effect to the advantage of one party or other.

(7) Taking persons into preventive custody to immobilize them from legitimate political activity in opposition to the party in power.

(8) Foisting false criminal cases against political functionaries for achieving political ends.

(9) Discretionary enforcement of law while dealing with public order situations, with emphasis on severity and ruthlessness in regard to persons opposed to the ruling party.

(10) Manoevring police intervention by exaggerating a non-cognizable offence or engineering a false complaint to gain advantage over another party in a situation which lies outside the domain of police action of the normal course.

(11) Preparation of malicious and tendentious intelligence report to facilitate action against an opponent.

He enumerates them in the context of giving some typical situations or matters in which pressure is brought to bear on the police by political, executive and other extraneous sources.

National Police Commission: 1977-81 too have expressed the same or similar views in their reports. When one compares these views with what he sees in the report of the Indian Police Commission: 1902-03, he feels that the situation was much better in the British rule. The intensity of wounded justice was not as cruel as it is seen in a 50 years old democracy now. Matters have gone from bad to worse. Police Commissions were appointed to cure the disease and the Indian Police Commission made recommendations to treat the disease. Nevertheless, what is seen now is that the cure has aggravated the disease to the extent that wounded justice administration spreads as an epidemic to many areas about which the British Commission (1902-03) could not even imagine during the colonial rule.

People and Police: Yesterday and Today

In a recently held conference, many police officers said: "The people are not cooperating"

"The people are not offering their willing participation"

"The people avoid the police and keep away".

I thought that there was no meaning in analyzing the causes of people's negative attitude. For, I knew that every police officer knew the causes. Then the question was: "If the people do not come to police, then what should the police do to get a positive attitude from the people?" There is a cliche-ridden saying: "If the mountain does not come to Mohammed, then Mohammed must go to the mountain". Applying the principle in police - citizen interactions, let the police think of how they can go to the people to get their cooperation.

The disease of people's negative attitude to police has a history of more than one century. For the Indian Police Commission: 1902-03 found that the people as a rule were not prepared to aid the police in investigation. The Commission observed that the reporting of crime was not wholly satisfactory.

The Commission noted further: "a police investigation always must entail some measure of worry and annoyance, that the prosecution of cases involves interruption of village work....and often also very considerable trouble and expense, and that those inducements to silence and neutrality have been greatly strengthened by the defective character of police and magisterial work". The observations made by the Indian Police Commission during 1902-03 hold good even today. Along with Dr. Alphonse L. Earayil, I made a study on the same issue and the observations of the study were published. We have analyzed the causes of people's negative approach to police and we did make many suggestions. Frustratingly enough, we do not find any interest or inclination on the part of the administrators to see that the suggestions and recommendations are meaningfully and purposively implemented.

Or, who is interested to improve police and police-citizen relations? The vested interests want to retain the police and their strength to their advantage. The British did so and they could succeed in making the people hostile to police or vice versa. The democracy's Governments which came into power from time to time did the same thing which the British did in so far as they wanted the police to retain their rule in the democracy. Of course, unlike the British, the democratically elected governments did not want the police to become hostile to people or vice versa. At the same time, many governments did not do anything to develop a closer relationship between the police and the people. At the same time, many politicians and ministers in government always said and they continue to say that the relationship between the police and the people must be smooth, healthier and nice. Their sincerity in saying so is at best suspicious and many impartial critics may even say that theirs is only platform gimmicks. Their hypocrisy is always proved by the fact that there exist no worthwhile plans and programmes for improving police - citizen interaction.

Truly, the Indian Police Commission: 1902-03 recommended that in every province, there should be a well equipped police training school for offering training to police officers of the rank of sub-inspectors. The Commission suggested that the trainees ought to be taught the *'manner in which police officers should conduct themselves towards the people*. God alone knows how did the British executed their Commission's decisions. Anyhow, the police behaviour towards the people was so loathsome and fear causing that the Central Committee on Police Training (1973) made many recommendations to improve police - community relations. The Committee also introduced many topics in the syllabus and insisted that the subject should be taught by case-study methods, role-playing methods, taking the trainees to live situations etc. The Committee also recommended inservice, orientation, re-orientation, special courses etc. for making an attitudinal change among police officers when they behave to the citizens in a democracy. It may be taken note of that the British training was such that the democratic India had to see that some *re-orientation* courses were to be introduced in police training institutions. Now, the police, people and the governments speak of *community policing* and one sees arguments *pro and contra* in introducing the same. The way the idea is executed is questioned by many. *Trial and Error* methods continue for enhancing police human relations with people. After the Committee on Police Training (1973), the National Police Commission: 1977-81 too made many recommendations for improving police - people relationship. The Committee on Police Reforms now at work too puts some questions on the same subject. It shows that the exercise which the Indian Police Commission:1902-03 started continues even today - even after a century since the police citizen relationship does not become enviable. If the relationship is strange, wounded justice may be resulted. Two days ago, a deputy commandant of an Armed Reserve told me: "Any hike in the pay of a constable/officer will not improve police citizen interaction". I asked him: 'Why?' Then he told me: "Bad behaviour or misbehaviour with the people is linked with many advantages and fortunes for the police. A bad behaviour brings corruption money and a misbehaviour brings many other fortunes". Yes, there is a point in what he said. On my way back from the Armed Reserve Camp, I thought : "Yes, there is a lot of truth in what the deputy commandant said". I continued to think: "Yes, any amount of training, counselling, advice may not be a substitute for corruption money and other advantages which bad behaviour or misbehaviour may guarantee". Certainly, the deputy commandant is right. For, '*what good behavior can't offer, bad behaviour offers and all is well that ends well*'. The repressive and oppressive police of the imperial rule with their loyalty to arms, ammunition, lathy power and muscles may be exerting its strength to make money, fortunes, luxury and advantages by being and becoming people unfriendly in police work. Some policemen/officers think that people unfriendly attitude and approaches yield better results in policing the society with a people friendly attitude. I doubt whether or not the people too think in the same way the policemen/officers think about police-citizen relationship!

State Security Commission and Wounded Justice

The National Police Commission: 1977-81 appointed by the Janata Government at the Centre examined the basic structure of the police and their statutory role to function as impartial, truthful and just executors of a law with morality, beyond interference by politicians, political parties or other extraneous sources. The National Police Commission, through their arm-chair speculations, recommended the appointment of a State Security Commission to exercise statutory control over the police which will be, according to the Police Commission, strictly held accountable to the State Security Commission for its performance under the law to serve public interest.

Nevertheless, the governments which came into power from time to time afterwards simply refused to implement the recommendations of the National Police Commission. The reasons are many for the rejection of the Commission's report and that is not the issue under discussion here. My book - *National Police Commission: Issues For Rethinking* - may help people to have an insight in the matter. At the same time, one may notice that police has never been free from political interference or politicians' interference. How did the politician come to the picture if the police could ensure just justice to the people? A sort of YIELD AND RULE policy has been seen by politicians among many police officers and it caused miscarriage of justice.

The Head of the Police Department - i.e., the Inspector General of Police as the post was then known in British India - could not get the required trust from many. There was no politician or political party during the colonial rule, yet the Indian Police Commission : 1902-03 said that the office of the Inspector General "should for the present ordinarily be held by a selected 'District Magistrate' because the training of a member of the Civil Service fits him better than a police officer to take broad views of administrative matters and to deal with intricate, difficult and important questions". What does it mean? There is a feeling among a section of the public that police officers, owing to their training and experience, develop a sort of *tunnel vision* to realities-that they fail to or refuse to take broad views of administrative matters. Whatever that be, the decisions taken by the police chief have a say in the administration of justice and certainly they decide the nature of justice.

The National Police Commission says that the public image and personality of the police chief are important in ensuring public confidence in the impartiality and effectiveness of the police. For this, the Commission has recommended a fixed tenure for the police chief. The Commission has also made certain conditions for the removal of the police chief appointed for a fixed tenure. To quote C.V. Narasimham once again : "While all State governments were prepared to implement some of the reforms of a relatively minor nature within the existing set up, none of them showed willingness to constitute a State Security Commission to insulate the police from interference from extraneous sources, political or otherwise. This is because of the reluctance of ruling parties in government to give up their exclusive control over the police. Even some of the police chiefs who had apparently climbed up ladder of promotions in service with political patronage seem to be unwilling to endorse the new system which would make the police accountable to multi-member body at the top, cutting across political lines. These senior officers have grown in a politicized system and seem to be happy with it! This is detrimental to public interest and the rule of law for the common good of all people". The observations made by C.V. Narasimham, no doubt, speak only one side of the story. There are other sides too. Political interference in police work alone is not - can not be - the sole cause of wounded justice administration. Sometimes, political interference becomes the sole cause for administering justice. Police officers themselves object to the new system and to call all who do so to be people apparently climbed up the ladder of promotions in service with political patronage seem to be uncharitable and against facts. Even in the British period, when there was no political interference, one takes note of wounded justice administration and precisely therefore one can not simply endorse the view that political interference alone is the root cause of wounded justice administration today. There is the human element - a human content - in every police decision and whenever the chief of police takes a fiat *attitude* to political interference , he fails to adhere to the age honoured principles of justice. Police officers have an affinity towards weapons and muscles power. If they are not controlled by a political leadership, then there is no meaning in having a Constitution and a democratic rule of government. It is not because there is political interference in police work that wounded justice is administered, but it is because the people at every level in the police hierarchy are prepared to yield to political interference - mostly for retaining their self interest and parochial advantages.

Once a director general of police said that police officers who have an integrity and character could just forget about any political influence in administration of justice. Then I asked him: "What do you mean?" He said: "If political pressure is exerted on A (the director general of police), he must just ignore it. What can the political leadership then do? He may be transferred. Still another director general of police have to be appointed. He too ignores the political pressure. He does things according to law. He may be transferred out and a third director general of police will be appointed. He too does the same thing".

"Will that be possible?" - I asked him.

"See, the political leadership or the ruling government can appoint only one from the Indian police service as the director general of police. If everyone in the Indian police service has an upright character and an integrity in approach, then nobody or no force on earth can exert undue influence on him" - he said.

Of course, there is a logic in what he says and he argues out his point well. The question is : "Is it possible to get such officers when there are people who expect party tickets to contest in elections ?" We have cases in which police chiefs contested in elections and have become MLA and MP in India.

In a western country the government enacted certain laws. The Supreme Court of that Country declared the laws to be unconstitutional. The government felt that the judges did so because they were not in favour of the government. Hence, the government fixed the upper age limit for retirement and saw to it that all judges retired on superannuation. Later, the same government appointed judges whom it thought to be favouring the government. Really, they were. The government subsequently passed the laws and then they were challenged in the Supreme Court. The newly appointed judges whom the government thought to be the partymen saw to it that they declared all the laws to be unconstitutional. The judges were above political considerations. They were men of character, integrity and justice mindedness. They assumed a different personality when they occupied the chairs of the judges in the Supreme Court. This is called just justice administration.

A director general of police who can rise to the position of the director general of police must assume a personality beyond his political affiliations so long as he adorns the chair of the director general of police. This is not seen and that is the reason why he becomes susceptible to political interference. The disease is in the director general of police and not at all in the political system. The disease becomes epidemic and spreads to all levels and that is the reason why people say that there is wounded justice administration at all levels.

Can the proposed State Security Commission make the director general of police to be a man of upright character, integrity and conscience? If not, wounded justice administration will be the after effect even in the new system. Wounded justice administration may take place at all levels and therefore the integrity and uprightness must be seen at all levels.

Police officers must be free in exercising their duties as per law and procedure established by law with an upright conscience and morality. Freedom, Sartre says, itself is the only enduring value. He continues saying that one must maintain his freedom in actions. It is always good and to abandon it is the one unforgivable evil. Whenever a police officer becomes vulnerable to political pressures, he abandons his freedom and thereby commits an unforgivable evil. His decisions, choices and actions make him what he is. In such a situation, he accepts full responsibility for his choices, actions and decisions. This is not seen among many police functionaries and the director general of police may not be an exception. A police officer who executes law in accordance to what he is told by the politicians, then he becomes faceless - a member of the mass and thereby paves the way for administering wounded justice. He does not take the responsibility for his choices, decisions and actions. Sartre again says: "And when we say that man is responsible for himself, we do not mean that he is responsible only for his own individuality, but that he is responsible for all men. When we say that man choose himself, we also mean that in choosing for himself, he choose for all men". A police officer - and not the politician - is responsible for his actions. When he does an act or takes a decision, he does so or takes a decision like that for others. And precisely therefore he has to be just and honest. For example, a police officer humiliates a man as he is forced by political pressures. When he humiliates a fellow citizen, he knows that he is doing something wrong. If he believes that it is the wrong thing to do so, then he must accept the fact that at the bottom of his choice, he alone chooses. Even if the pressure comes from the political head quarters, government, departmental higher ups, he can not evade his won responsibility for administering wounded justice to that man. Blaming political pressure is an escape mechanism. There can not be any legal justifications, moral rationalizations or political explanations for the evil he does. If he considers that humiliating a man is a wrong act, it is only he who chooses so and therefore he alone is responsible and guilty. He is free and he is freedom in such situations.

The story of Indian police shows that many policemen/ officers have done many things and thereby they have administered wounded justice. This is seen among the policeman in the British past and even in the democratic present. Whenever they did wrong things, they wanted to put the blame on others and in a democracy, they could very well do so by blaming political pressure. The politicians are everybody's property and the police found them to be the best for blame and certainly, the blame could serve their own interests. Having tasted the immense advantage of having politicians brought to police administration, the police functionaries continue to say that wounded justice takes place owing to excessive political interference!.

8

Wounded Justice: National Police Commission–Before and After

Thirty years after India became independent i.e., in 1977- Government of India appointed a National Police Commission to better the police system. The terms of reference to the Commission show that the Government wanted, among other things - to make the police a justice friendly organization. The Commission made extensive study and research, held discussions with many experts, visited many countries, organized seminars for several years until atlast the Commission was asked to wind up the work. The Commission submitted eight reports and they contained several recommendations. The reports of the Commission have become documents of history and the Commission itself was made a part of police history.

Between 1947 and 1977, many States in India appointed their own police commission to study the police functionings and to suggest measures to improve the police system. These States level commissions were more concerned about the pay, housing, recruitment, training, posts, promotions, discipline etc. and less concerned about the administration of fair justice or making the police more people friendly. The Chairmen of some of the State level commissions were *about to retire* police officers who knew well that they were appointed just for making them engaged till they retired on superannuation. In some States, the reports of such Commissions were not taken seriously either by the State Governments or by the policemen/officers or by the people. They too, in some States, have become part of police history and some enterprising research scholars might look into such historical records kept in the archieves for the purpose of writing a paper or a dissertation. In spite of the independence for India and amidst these State level police commissions, the police system designed by the British continued to function without any change under the Indian Police Act-1861. Political parties, political leaders, governments, police administrators who ruled the country and administered justice found the police a convenient force to serve their parochial interests. No one including the hierarchy took any interest to reform the police by fundamentally restructuring it to fit the police in accordance to democracy's principles and people's aspirations. Of course, the 1977 National Police Commission examined the police system and functionings and made some recommendations which remain only as recommendations in papers and exactly therefore the police in India today is essentially the police in India which functioned under the Indian Police Act-1861. The advantages and disadvantages of the Police Act-1861 are seen today as they were existence prior to the appointment of the National Police Commission-1977. In the resolution which accepted the recommendations of the Indian Police Commission: 1902-03, it is seen: "Of all the branches of the public service in India, the police, by its history and traditions, is the most backward in its character". Is that observation valid today? The above resolution concluded: "The reconstruction of the police is, indeed, merely a step towards the improvement of the administration of criminal justice in India. Success in that higher aim will depend not only on the qualifications and training of the force, but even more on the honest cooperation of the people themselves in the work of reform". The attitude and approach to the police, to administration of criminal justice, to public cooperation etc. which the British had were praiseworthy – and most unfortunately we did not see any such attitude and approach among Indian Political leaders, police administrators, democratic Governments till today. Look at Lord Curzon's observation: "a government which places the preservation of internal order and the detection, prevention and punishment of crime in soiled or incompetent hands can not escape reproach". How said it had been/is that no one who occupied-occupies high positions in democratic India thought-thinks as Lord Curzon thought about a century ago!

National Police Commission and Wounded Justice

"Custodial deaths and police misconduct towards persons in detention, particularly women, are causing much concern to the public," - says National Police Commission in the first report. This is a frank confession and a plain repeating of what Torture Commission said in 1855 and what the Indian Police Commission said in 1902-03. The story is repeated that a custodial death has been reported in the press just a few days ago. According to the report of the National Human Rights Commission (1996-97), there were as many as 136 deaths during 1995-1996 and 188 deaths during 1996-1997. Including those died in judicial custody, the custodial deaths went up to 444 and 888 respectively - a doubling in the total number of custodial deaths. Human rights Commissions award heavy compensation to the next of kin of the deceased and severe penalty is imposed. Yet the tragedy continues...the misfortune takes place! Is it a curse? The National Police Commission in the first report says: "An effective check against this malady is the provision for a mandatory judicial inquiry into all such complaints of custodial death or police high-handedness of a serious nature". Will it work?

Immanuel Kant says: "Always act on that maxim which can at the same time be made a universal law of conduct". However good may be the recommendation of the National Police Commission establishing a working mechanism for involving the district judiciary for ensuring an effective check against custodial violence/death, the recommendation will have no value unless the men behind the causing of custodial violence/ deaths change. In my judgement, the change lies in the deep disposition of the heart of the police officers - in their value system – in their upright conscience. Police officers are first of all human beings. They are rational and should have morality. They have self-esteem, a dignity and worth of their own. They must accept that others - including the suspects, arrestees and detinues have dignity, worth and rights. To quote again Immanuel Kant: "Act in such a way that you always treat humanity, whether in your own person or in the person of another, never simply as a means but always at the same time as an end". Humanity is in everyone and all persons under police custody have it. Honour it and never treat other persons as means - means to achieve a conviction for him from a court of law. If he/she is a suspect in a crime, he/she is the end - *an end* which needs correction and rehabilitation. In one instance, a sub-inspector told his subordinates in the police station: "I want the suspect to be produced before magistrate tomorrow. The magistrate will not accept dead bodies". The question here is: "Is the suspect an end or a means to an end?"

The police in India, I think could consider - even now consider - the suspects, arrestees and detinues only as a means to an end. What is that end? Many policemen/officers do not know it even today. This is, perhaps, one of the reasons for the policemen/police department to become unpopular. In 1904, the Inspector General of Police in Madras wrote: "Always unpopular, the department has become more than ever an easy, and as it were an authorized target for aspersion both in the press and in the courts". Even today, there are a number of policemen/officers who hold a similar view and it means that they simply refuse to see things in broad day light. By employing torture/third degree methods on the suspects/interrogated, the police may be able to get a confession, identify a culprit and obtain a conviction from the court. Does it mean everything in police work? Do the police have any public trust or trust from the courts? What is the meaning in the increase of custodial deaths? A century ago - in 1904, the police realized that they lost trust from the courts and people. What did they do to achieve the lost trust? Nothing! What are they doing now? Nothing! I want to quote from the Administrative report (Madras, 1904) : "One of the most apparent of these is that the courts have undoubtedly become more suspicious of police work and police cases, and that convictions are harder to obtain, while another is that, with diminished credit and prestige, the influence of the police has declined throughout the country and the respect, in which it has held, has decreased, with the inevitable further result of diminished efficiency". Has the situation improved now? If not, what are the reasons?

Today, many accuse the politicians and the political set up as the sole reasons for deterioration in police service or decline in police values. It is easy to do so and by doing so, one can escape his responsibility for doing injustice. Is the political pressure responsible for causing custodial violence/custodial deaths? In no case so far registered for lockup deaths, politicians are seen as the accused. Yet, the National Police Commission writes in their second Report: "There is very urgent need to insulate the police from political and other extraneous interference, which is now making police performance appear very partisan and corrupted". The Commission says: "appear very partisan and corrupted" and the people ask: "only appear? Not actual?" and the Commission wants to eradicate this evil by instituting a State Security Commission!. One may remember that no external force will or can cause an internal change unless the pressured wants to change themselves. The issue involves morality and moral convictions. If politics and politicians are unwanted and unwarranted in a democracy, then democracy will cease to function. What guarantee can the police give to people that they will not administer wounded justice even without any political interference? During 1900, there was no political interference in police work, but police administration was far away from being satisfactory. Why?

In 1936, Lord Linlithgow in his message to the police said: "To all branches of the police in India, I give my greetings.

The services that you perform are essential to the welfare of the public, for your duty requires that you should be friends and protectors of all persons who are concerned, within the law of the land, to proceed upon their lawful occasions.

I am confident that in your relations with the public, you will see at all times to discharge your duties with firmness, tact and impartiality.

You should rest assured that in the performance of your arduous duties, sometimes difficult, at moments dangerous, and always delicate, you may count upon my steady support.

Your welfare will at all times be my anxious care".

The question is: "How many directors general of police and superior police officers will be able to or willing to ensure their steady support to their subordinates today?" Another question is: "How many senior officers have the anxious care about which Lord Linlithgow spoke to the members of the police department. If the *steady support* and anxious care do not come from the superior ranks in police, necessarily politicians will come to aid the police just like they come to aid the members of the public. Disowning the subordinates by the superiors has become a problem now a days - so much so that the subordinates want political patronage for their existence and survival - so much so that the superior want political support for the continued survival in police department. Political interference in police work thus becomes a *necessary evil* without which no fair justice is possible - feel the people. If torture is an evil in police work, political interference too is an evil. If corruption is an evil in police, then political corruption is an evil. In spite of the political interference in the democracy as it is seen today, National Human Rights Commission finds that Custodial torture/death continues to be an evil in police work. How to get out of the evil? Can the police claim that all they do at present are for administration of fair justice? Can the police claim that all they do at present are unintentional acts or as mere oversight? Can the police claim that all that they do today are done out of necessity? Can the police claim that they are innocent in everything they do? The advocates who argue for the police can not silence their accusers saying that the police commit atrocities on people as they are not free to act owing to political interference?

National Police Commission in the third Report says: "Economically disadvantaged, socially deprived and weaker sections in society are often the victims of high handedness by the affluent and powerful groups in the community. Police tend to ignore the plight of such victims and refrain from taking any positive action against the aggressors". Why? The National Police Commission continues, "The power of arrest presently available to the police is often misused to harass and humiliate persons in several situations, prompted by malafide considerations". Why? A sample survey conducted by the National Police Commission revealed that "a large number of arrests made by police are ultimately unjustified". Why? The Commission says further: "....harmless persons who need not be arrested at all are often arrested and even got remanded to custody on trumped up materials in police records which ultimately may not go to court at all". Why? All these show the extent and intensity of wounded justice administration. One can not blame that all these malpractices take place merely and solely because there is the political interference. What is the responsibility of police then? Are they not legally and morally responsible for their acts? Don't they have any principles of behaviour? Don't they have a responsibility to collect data before they act? The police have their own methods of data collection. They can eliminate what is not necessary from the data so collected by them. They can as well as act legally with an upright conscience. They try to put the entire blame to political interference. This is unwarranted and uncharitable and precisely therefore works as the root cause of wounded justice administration. In the British past, the police blamed the British Government for what they did wrongly and unjustly and in the democratic present, they blame the democratically elected governments, politicians and political interference. Blaming others is not a solution for wounded justice administration.

Sir Edmund Cox said that the labours of the Police Commission: 1902-03 made no difference or improvements to the then existed police system. He said further: "When a crime had been committed in a village, the police investigation that ensues is likely in the nature of things to cause annoyance to a number of people". Even today the same thing happens. National Police Commission said many things and recommended a lot of changes in the then existed police functioning. But, even after nearly two decades since the commission made its recommendations, the situation in police continues to be the same which existed before the Commission's report came into light. There were many recommendations which cound be implemented if there was a change in the attitude of police. This does not take place. Of course, the Governments that came into power in India did not implement the recommendations of the Commission. But, what prohibited the individual policemen/ officers to change their attitudes/approaches? For example in the fourth report of the National Police Commission reads: "In the existing scheme of things, persons who are examined by the police as witnesses in respect of an occurrence do not have the facility of knowing how exactly their statements have been recorded by the police. This peculiar position in law enables dishonest police officers to make indifferent or incorrect record of statements of witnesses which ultimately affects the disposal of cases in court trial later". The National Police Commission had recommended amendments to sections 161 and 162, Code of Criminal Procedure - 1973 and I do not know how far or how much the proposed amendments would effect corresponding changes in the dishonesty of police investigation. If dishonesty is the problem, then that must be cured. If a crime investigator thinks that everything is permitted and he has neither behind him nor before him any human values - neither above him nor around him any luminous realm of justice - then he becomes the rule and in such a situation, wounded justice will be resulted. Such policemen were there in the 19th and 20th century and they make the police department a department administering wounded justice. Dinsha Edulji Watcha said in the beginning of the last century in an interesting pamphlet titled *Police Reforms* that the police was a "rotten organization which purported to protect life and property and detect true crimes".

Police, Social Justice and Administration of Wounded Justice

What is the meaning and purpose of policing a democracy? This concern has been seen among many civic minded people in India. History repeats and that is what the people see when they study the story of police. What the police commissions - state level or otherwise - saw in the past have been found repeating, sometimes in a deeper and wider way. Now, the Government of India has appointed a Committee for Police Reforms and the Committee asks the same questions which earlier Commissions have asked hitherto. The National

Police Commission finds: "Police are now a days required to investigate offences under several Acts which are in the category of social legislation. In many cases of this kind, the police are seen exercising their powers under the law for making searches and arrests merely for harassing and humiliating persons who are generally law abiding and against whom complaints may have come up from disgrunted elements in society". Harassment and humiliation by police has been seen ever since the police started functioning. There seems to be no solutions although all the police commissions make recommendations which according to them will put an end to humiliation and harassment. But, history shows that the remedies suggested do not cure the disease.

Harassment and humiliation have become a part of police sub-culture! The police service has a meaning in a democracy - in a society. It has a purpose and that purpose is nothing but administration of justice in a fair and human rights friendly way. Police service has a meaning only if the service is rendered without making any discrimination to sex, caste, class and status. Often, the poor and the helpless are harassed and humiliated. Police must have a moral meaning. The moral meaning is marked by a greater sensitivity to individual's rights and social welfare. So long as this is not seen, it is just not possible to ensure social justice to people.

Police over the years have developed an idea that they could be the measure of all things and they thought that the people appreciated what they did. People did not approve of many things which the police did and they included harassment, victimization, humiliation, use of torture, coercion etc. It was too late for the police to learn that the people were keeping away from them, but by the time they understood it, the distance between the police and the people became very large. Some policemen/officers even liked them to be called *lions* and *tigers* by the people, but today no one likes to be called (nicknamed) so. Earlier, the people were illiterate and the policemen too. Now people are educated and the policemen can not but become more cultured to behave in a cultured way. This is a reason, no doubt, why the *tigers*, *leopards* and *lions* are vanishing today from the police department. People admire the police when they do good things, but they reproach the police when they commit bad things. Immediately after the Ayodya event - i.e., demolition of the Babri-Masjid in Uttar Pradesh, there took place some chaos/law and order problems. In connection with one such problem, the police in a south Indian State behaved very calmly and firmly. The State Government immediately granted a huge amount of money to be distributed as gifts to all policemen for their meritorious work. A study was conducted to elicit the views of the general public and it showed that the people were happy to offer gifts to police. They appreciated the Government for the nice gesture shown to the police. At the same time, the same people accuse the Government when custodial deaths are reported or unbecoming behaviour is shown by the policemen. Policemen include the constables up to the director general of police. I am of the firm view that the policeman can prevent wounded justice, but he does not; or the wishes to prevent it but he can not. What is the reality? Certainly, the policeman can prevent it, but he does not want it. Why? That is a long story and that is what the Police Commissions have written so far. Police is created necessarily for the best end. They are given pistols, lathies, power and authority etc. and all these are provided necessarily for the best end. If they have misused them, it means that they do not want to prevent wounded justice administration.

Anandswarup Gupta, in the introduction of his book, The *Police of India: 1861-1947* writes: "But, as a legacy, Independent India received a police force with a very small Indian leadership and a subordinate body, which had been studiously trained in the use of brute force and in which extortion, corruption and malpractices had been tolerated with a callous indifference to the welfare and the dignity of the Indian citizen and had been allowed to acquire the sanctity of tradition; a system of supervision and control which prevented the development of professionalism in the force and was antagonistic to the establishment of the rule of law; a body of criminal laws which was hardly conducive to an effective control of crime and criminals; and a totally ineffective machinery for the security of the rural areas". What more one needs to see that wounded justice is administered?

Rule of Law and Justice

Rule of law is fundamental to a democracy. Rule of law does not mean a ruthless enforcement of law. In Kesavananda Bharathi's Case (W.P.No. 135 of 1970 dated 24.04.1973, A.I.R., 1973, S.C. 1461), the basic structure of the Constitution of India has been spelt out. They are —

(1) Supremacy of the Constitution

(2) Republican and democratic form of Government

(3) Secular character of the Constitution

(4) Separation of power among the legislature, the executive and the judiciary

(5) Federal Character of the Constitution

Police functions under the Constitution and the laws made thereunder. Wounded justice administration had no scope under the Constitution and the laws made thereunder. Indian Police Act - 1861, of course, was one which came into existence before the Constitution of India came into force. But, any provision which is against the Constitution is null and void.

Police have to bear in mind that they have to look into two aspects when they administer justice - i.e., the rule of law and the rule of justice. The rule of law must be ensured keeping the rule of justice in mind. It is here we see the role of legal mindedness, moral mindedness, upright conscience, human formation, human rights, human values, human consideration, humaneness, humanity, human face, human justice, human laws etc. playing for administering justice to people.

9

Wounded Justice:

Philosophies and Principles

There are a lot of rules and laws to guide the police, but one sees that the police unquestioningly accept their own practices as right. Human rights laws have come into being, but some police officers find it extremely difficult to deviate from their practices so far followed. A few of the police functionaries do condemn the human rights laws. They think that a practice in police gets developed during a period of time– by trial and error methods - and if that is so the practices become very sacred laws for the police to follow in their work situations. If third degree methods have proved to be an effective method to find out the truth in crime investigation then they can not be just thrown out by saying that they are human rights unfriendly. If a man can violate the human rights of others by committing crimes, then there is nothing wrong in police violating the human rights of the crime-order. No doubt, this is retribution - i.e., eye for eye and tooth for tooth principle - in police work. What is the illegality in becoming human rights unfriendly in cases that deserve retributive approaches? They argue that something is good if it works well and human rights unfriendly approaches work well in police investigation.

Legal Relativism

What makes a thing legally good or bad? Some police officers ask this question. They ask: "is there anything good or bad in police work?" Police job, they think, is the police traditions and practices. The democratic police in India had a long tradition and practice of British policing in India. Immediately after the independence in India in 1947, the police thought that they were doing everything in the right way. There was nobody to teach them the right and wrong in a democracy. The police strategies during an imperialist regime could not be made the strategies in a democratic rule. What was right for the British police was right simply because it enabled them to prosper well in the colonial India. Certainly, they were not right for the democratic India. What was good for the British then was good for them because it worked well during the British regime. It served their self-interests. Police might have been the measure of all things for the British. They thought that the real measure of legally right or wrong - of good or evil - was actually the extent to which their interests and desires were furthered. The police were then accountable only to the British Government in power, but today the police are accountable to the people in the democracy. The British enacted the laws and interpreted them in the way they wanted. This was called legal relativism and it could afford to offer only wounded-justice to the people. The legal relativism continued to dominate the police thinking even after India became independent. This was, probably, the reason why the police could not divorce themselves from human rights unfriendly attitudes till recently - till the Protection of Human Rights Act - 1993 was passed. Even today, some police officers are reluctantly accepting human rights laws and some others openly oppose them. Those who advocate retributive approaches to crime-doers belong to such category of police functionaries. They need more information and enlightening to become people's police in a democracy. Legal relativism may offer self-satisfactions, quick results, short-run hedonism to police functionaries, but they will be condemned as most obnoxious and undemocratic in the long run.

Legal Skepticism

If the police accept legal relativism, then there can not be anything *right* and *wrong* in law, For everything will be relative to the police officer. For example, suppose a police officer resorts to torture on a criminal, X by name and he does not use it to another, Y by name, then, what is the standard by which one may decide on the *right and wrong* in the use of torture? If *torturing* of X is legally right, then *not torturing* Y is legally wrong. They can not go hand in hand. If a course of action-here, the use of torture - is really a right thing in law, then it must be right always and everywhere. There is no question of employing double standards in justice administration. If the police do a particular thing just because it is a short cut for success, - or to reach the destination without taking pain-, then such a course of action is accepted not because it is legally right, but because it serves the self-interests of police officers. Anything done for serving the self-interest of police functionaries and not for serving the ends of justice administration will have no enduring significance. To pretend that illegal strategies are resorted to for administering just justice is nothing but hypocrisy in administration of justice.

The police have well written laws and procedures. When there is a written law, there is no scope for adopting *police practices* for reaching the destination quickly. When the Indian Penal Code, Code of Criminal Procedure, Human Rights laws disfavour the use of third degree methods, what is the purpose of bringing police practices and short cut methods to justify police acts which are illegal? Police thinking and their conduct must be guided by the existing laws and the international consensus on the subject. There is no scope for any legal skepticism there. What are the laws for administration of justice? They must be employed in spirit and in letters. If the laws enacted by the British in India are against the international thinking on the subject, then the international law must prevail.

Legal Realism

There is a feeling that the laws are enforceable against the enforceables. Petty thieves are caught and great ones are respected. Mustard seeds are seen and elephants are not. The police as an organization is very great, but each policeman as an individual is very weak. Some criminals are more powerful than the individual policeman including the director general of police. Some people think that *might is right* in justice administration and in some situations. Individual criminals become mightier than the individual policeman/mammoth police organization. He may mould the law to his interest.

Can we say that everything the police do in connection with crime investigation is right? No, we can not. No police officer will dare to say so. Police may do many things as per law or as per instructions from above or as per influences/ temptations etc. people obey the police as they have no option. Laws are made by those who are in power and both of them do it for their own interest. What happened to the police in British India? The police functions and law enforcement for nearly one hundred and fifty years in India were based upon the power of the British to maintain themselves here. Even after the independence of the nation, the police have been misused by the governments which have come into power from time to time. What happened to justice administration during the internal emergency during 1976-1977? Police misused their powers and there were a lot of criticisms against the police.

What types of penal laws are enforced in India? The question is asked by some police officers themselves. The penal laws are very antique and they were enacted in 1860 by the

British, primarily to serve their interests in India. The concept of crime was different then and the same laws are enforced here even now. What earthly use is there? If the British who were powerful then could manage and manipulate law enforcement then in India, the politicians, the powerful and the affluent can manage and manipulate the penal laws today in India. Some police officers really feel that they are made victims of this manipulation. This is what they mean by saying "Legal Realism".

Self-Centered Individualism

There is a view that every policeman/officer seeks his own interests without any regard to the enforcement of law or justice administration. Such people have no morality or legal ideal. The number of policemen/officers who have made fortunes through their job may not be small or insignificant. The view that the crime investigator manages and manipulates many things for serving his self-interests may not be always wrong. If that is true, then the police can administer only "wounded justice" to people. For them, *justice administrations* are nice words to hear and are good means to make fortunes in life. Every individual has moral, legal, religious and social dimensions and they, among other things, make him what he is in justice administration. If they make him to misuse his powers and police authority just to serve his self-centered individualism, then wounded justice will be the outcome.

Society-Centered Individualism

Different from the self-centered individualism, some police officers entertain a society centered individualism. They consider society more important than the individual and any police work for the society has an individual dimension for them. Charity with a hook-likewise, they do a lot of things for society, but their work will have a hook for their advantage.

They may misuse their power or abuse their authority and their argument will be that they do so for the larger interests of the society. On an ultimate analysis, one may find that they have some individual motives for the actualization of which they need social objectives and high sounding words. Politicians resort to this strategy and they call it "*service*" to society. Instances have been reported that some police officers catch hold of illicit liquor sellers for the benefit to the society and they secretly connive with liquor Mafia groups to make fortunes. They do so without any guilt consciousness and they call it "justice administration".

Policemen/officers may commit wrongs - may be, by mistake of law or mistake of fact. This is understandable. Nevertheless, knowing that something is bad or wrong and then doing it is not praiseworthy. Why does he do so? For example, use of epithets during a V.I.P.'s visit. He does so because it is advantageous to him (to others too sometimes). Society-centered individualism has been responsible for carving out a poor image of police-bringing disgrace to the service. Knowing that such activities will bring disgrace to self and to police service, some police officers involve in doing so. This is called self-deception. A Code of Conduct for policemen/officers is not, something, imposed on them by an external power/authority, rather it contains the principles of conduct designed to help them to administer just justice to people and to themselves.

Personal and Social Morality of Policemen/Officers

Personal and social morality, Socrates (470 -399 B.C) said, were but two aspects of one larger whole. In police, some believe that the personal life of a policeman/officer is different from his social life. How? There are policemen/officers who gamble, who womanize, who drink intoxicating liquors, who lead an immoral life and they claim that they are perfect men in their official life! How can they be? A policeman/officer is a human being and he is a part of the larger society. He can not have two faces - one face in the department and another face in society. A policeman/officer must be a law observer before he becomes a law enforcer. Whenever he exercises authority/power over the lives of others, he must do so with his personal and social morality. Police exercise their powers to build a just society and thereby to shape the conscience of the community.

After India became independent in 1947, the democracy's police were in no mood to change their old police strategies. They continued to work in the colonial fashion and that was without any social dimension and police accountability to the public in a democracy. Even today, allegations are there that the police have not adopted democracy's policing and principles of policing a democracy. This is one of the reasons for the prevalence of *wounded justice* administration in India.

Can a crime-free society make the people happy? Evidence in hand proves that there is no crime-free society. A crimeless or crime-free society is an impossibility and precisely therefore, there must be police and policing the society. Just like agriculture, education, hospitals etc., police too is a necessity for a society. Views and opinions change as to how must the police work in society. No doubt, they must behave in a human rights friendly way.

Some police officers think that it is just not possible to be human rights friendly always in police service. It is Aristippus, a wandering Sophist of Cyrene (ca.430-350 B.C.) who said that the pursuit of pleasure and the avoidance of pain were the two driving forces in the behaviour of all creatures. Police, just like all others in society, want to have the pursuit of pleasure and the avoidance of pain. Can they get them when they administer just justice? They will get them only when and if only they administer just justice. Whenever they administer or assist in administering wounded justice, they do not (ought not) get pleasure and avoid pain. Wounded justice consists of unjust/unethical acts which offer pleasures of the senses for the time being, and certainly, they damage the reputation and good name of the police department. In a democracy, pleasures mean the pleasures of the society and also of the individuals. Justice administration, therefore, must be for ensuring pleasure to society and to individuals and in such a system, there is little or no scope for administration of human rights unfriendly police justice.

Legal Responsibility for Wounded Justice

Some police officers tell that the responsibility for *wounded justice* administration must be shared by all sub-systems in justice administration. Police have a responsibility, but they do not have the full responsibility. If failures are there, the entire police system must be blamed. The individual police investigator has only a part - responsibility as he forms only a part of the entire system. Everyone has a tendency to blame the police as the principal or the only agency responsible for administration of wounded justice. Those who blame the investigating officer do not move their little fingers to help him in some way to better the system. Police investigators at times quote a stanza of Rubaiyat and console themselves -

> ***"Strange, is it not? that of the myriad's who***
> ***Before us puss'd the door of Darkness through,***
> ***Not one returns to tell us of the Road,***
> ***Which to discover we must travel too"***

And what to do? The judges, the press, the public, the jurists, the lawyers, the police brethren, the accused, the victims and the myriad's who blame the investigating officers do not tell them of the road to travel to administer just justice:

Pleasure-Pain Approach

Democracy accepts the greatest amount of pleasure and the least pain for maximum number of people. In order to ensure them, crimes have to be controlled and the police are the control mechanism. Some police officers argue that infliction of pain to a minority of people is justified for the larger interest of the society. Thus, human rights unfriendly approach to crime-doers is fully justified as it ensures the greatest amount of pleasure to the largest number of people. But, the international community is against this approach as it can not accept such a crude approach which guarantees only short-lived pleasures that cost too much. "Let one thousand criminals go unpunished; no innocent man must be punished" - this is an accepted dictum in jurisprudence. If that is so, causing pain to people to put down crimes before the crime is proved against them after a fair trial is not justified. A police service which is human rights friendly is a cultured service. The pleasure of having a society with reduced number of crimes must be guided by reason and not by passion. In such a situation, third degree methods and other enforcement crimes by police have no relevance and scope. After becoming human rights unfriendly, how do policemen/officers feel? Do they have pleasures of the mind? Or do they have only the pleasures of the body? If they do not experience mental tranquility, then the service ceases to have any meaning in any society. Epicurus once wrote:

"Even though pleasure is our first and native goal, for that reason we do not choose every pleasure whatsoever but of times pass over many pleasures when a greater annoyance issues from them...not all pleasure is worthy to be chosen". In a democracy, the police can not choose all sorts of pleasure to ensure pleasure in society.

A man, being a human being, can become a policeman and not at all a *police-animal.* Policeman, while he renders service to society, can not render it in an animal - like way. A policeman must be able to conquer his animal instincts and the success goes to him if he is able to become human rights friendly in his attitudes and approaches.

Science and Police

Many people argue that science will aid the police in their work, nevertheless, many police officers do not subscribe to such a view. Science has many limitations and police work is not 2+2 = 4. Pure science does not and can not put down crimes in society and ensure fair justice. Police can not subscribe to the view that science is everything in police work. Human freedom is something beyond 2+2=4. *Destiny* is another thing the science can not explain. Some crimes are committed by people by chance; some others out of necessity; some others by pre-planning and calculation; some others by victimological compulsions; some others by multiple causation factors and how can 2+2=4 approach explain all these? There is no simple or single approach to all sorts of criminals. To some, a human rights friendly approach may become successful and to some others, it may not. To some, torture may yield good results and to some others, it may not. Hence there is no single or simple approach which is purely scientific in police work. Human rights laws are good principles, but how can they be enforced scientifically? Hence, some police officers say that those who make the human rights laws in their own view have no concern at all with the mortal policemen/officers and they do not experience directly or indirectly the policemen's day to day conducts. They have very little knowledge about the ground realities in police work. It is true that many human rights activists and advocates of human rights have little or no knowledge of ground realities in police work; nevertheless, they think that the policemen must be controlled in their activities. Seeing and studying what the policemen do today, they feel that restrictions are necessary for controlling the policemen. If they are not handcuffed by human rights laws, certainly they misuse their power and abuse their authority. Also, they see that many police officers/men who are human rights friendly render enviable service to humanity. Of course, 2+2=4 principle in pure mathematics or science can not work as such in police work; nevertheless, the police can very well apply the principles in social sciences/police science to police situations. But, they do not have recourse to principles in psychology in their work. The result has been very dangerous to human welfare and happiness. This must be avoided and the policemen/officers must be psychological and scientific if they want to avoid administering *wounded justice* to people. Indian mystical revelations too support the view that one must be human rights friendly in his approaches. Hence, it is to the spirit of Indian culture and civilization of justice that the police be scientific and psychological in everything.

Visibility of Police Actions

Some of the police actions are visible and some are invisible to the public. Administration of wounded justice is fully visible or partly visible to the public. To cause deterrence among the public, it is argued by some police officers, that the police can afford to become human rights unfriendly in some situations - nay - they say that the police must be human rights unfriendly. Deterrence purposefully caused by the police is very visible to the public and that alone works as a control of criminal behaviour in society.

The questions are: "should the police become deterrent in a democracy?" "If they must become deterrent, how should they become?" "Can they become retributive?" Studies show that deterrence for deterrence' sake is not deterrent at all - and likewise, retribution shows only the vindictive nature of human animality. There is a greater greatness in the greatness of becoming non-retributive in police work. It is the certainty of police action and not the severity of police action that deters the people from committing crimes. Deterrence and retribution have helped more to administer *wounded justice* than to administer *fair justice*.

Altruistic Hedonism and Police

The police claim that the very purpose of police service is altruistic hedonism. The welfare of the fellow men - that is a desirable thing if the police can achieve the goal. In order to ensure altruistic hedonism, the police may have to cause pain to some and that pain is a necessary '*evil*' in police administration. Some people or vested interests may call it *wounded justice*, but in reality, those evils are necessary for establishing altruistic hedonism. How far can one agree with this argument?

A crime-doer, no doubt, is one who disregards others' welfare and therefore, let him suffer the consequence of his action. The question is: "should it be before a verdict of guilt from a court of law?" A criminal as per the existing international consensus, enjoys human rights and how can the police violate human rights laws when they deal with criminals? They can not and therefore, causing pain by police hands before a judgement declaring the accused to be guilt in the name of altruistic hedonism is not justified. Let the police deal with crime-doers in a human rights friendly way. It will be simply appreciated and loved by the people. On the contrary, let the police deal with a crime-doer in a human rights unfriendly manner in the name of altruistic hedonism, then it will be adversely commented and criticized. Appreciation of police work follows as the natural consequence of right police strategies and adverse criticisms follow as the natural consequence of wrong police strategies. We, often, listen to adverse criticisms and the altruistic hedonism does not come into picture at all when people adversely criticize the police. Whenever the police administer wounded justice or administer injustice, people resent them in loud voice. Altruistic hedonism via wounded justice administration should never be the motivating forces in police work.

Philosophers in Police

Policemen/officers get any number of opportunities to directly witness human miseries. If they have a human heart, many of them can become good philosophers. Having exposed to such human situations, how can't the police be good philosophers? Some have sublime philosophies, but they do not tell them even to their close friends. Every policeman is an intelligent and social human being or if he is not, then he must be. More than the pleasures of the senses, justice means or must mean something that is or can be given only by human beings and not by animals. Custodial violence, custodial rapes or custodial deaths etc. take place in police lockups and no human philosophy can explain such atrocities. A criminal however cruel he may be, has a right to be safe in police custody. Police may be able to silence people who disagree with them. But, it is not justice - rather is wounded justice and no police philosopher can give a rational explanation to such cruelties on man in police custody. Policemen themselves say that they must be human and every time very human in all approaches and attitudes. Epictetus, a Stoic philosopher in Rome (55-135 AD) said: "It is the duty of philosophers to superintend as far as they can all mankind and see what they do, how they live, what they neglect contrary to their duty". In that sense, every policeman is a philosopher and he occupies a public office not to tyrannize people, but to render human service to all who need his valuable service. I think that there is no service in today's democratic rule that is more talked of and criticized or less understood than the police.

Policeman, the Captain of the Situation and Master of Crime-control

Stoics said that *man is the captain of his soul and the master of his fate.* Almost a similar view is taken by some policemen/officers on police responsibility in society. 'Policeman is the captain of the situation' - is this view correct? They think so by taking the role of police in law and order situations. Management of law and order is not everything in policing and therefore, the view is faulty. Even in a law and order situation, the policeman is not the captain as he is accountable for everything he does there. Is the policeman the master of crime-control. This too is not a correct view, for, police is just an agency - may be an important agency - of social control. They can not control crimes alone, rather they have to work in liaison with other crime-control agencies. Therefore, it is the responsibility of the police to see that they administer justice to people in a just way without assuming too much about their role in society. Police may administer or aid to administer wounded justice because they entertain false notions about their role. The view they take may mislead them and one reason why they think so is because of the false notion they inherited from the British past. In the British rule, the police was a repressive force and they could afford to be the captain or the master as the case might be. People had no option other than yielding to their repressive rule. Today, in a democracy, the police is no longer the master or captain.

Administration of *wounded justice* has a linkage with the attitude the police take to people. Whether a particular strategy of action is good or evil with respect to a particular individual depends heavily upon the attitude which individual police officers/men have towards people. Allegations are there that some police officers are unjust to the poor and the needy, to the women and other handicapped in society. This is so because of the special and peculiar attitude which the police functionaries have. On the contrary, some other police officers/men are accused of showing leniency towards the rich, affluent or influential. This too is wounded justice and is due to the faulty attitude which police officers/men have towards such people. All depends upon how do policemen/officers take things or how do they make of them and certainly they depend upon the policemen/officers themselves. One's attitude towards the suspects/accused in a crime can be retributive and that is the precise reason why the Central Committee on Police Training instituted by Government of India recommended that there should be special courses organized for effecting attitudinal change among policemen/officers.

Some police officers say that the antique and time worn laws in India make them to administer wounded justice. It may be true, yet the fact remains that the people behind the laws and their enforcement have a lot to do - to decide - to execute when they administer justice.

Problems of Wounded Justice

Whether one likes it or not, administration of *wounded justice* is a reality and the police is one of the powerful agencies responsible for it. Employment of torture, manipulation of records, illegal arrests, informal detentions etc. are sometimes seen in police administration of justice and certainly, they inflict manifold miseries and sufferings upon hundreds of thousands of people - helpless citizens - in the Country. Can we say that they are just the *ills of administration of justice* and then forget all about those ills? Can we just say that they are the necessary evils in an antiquated justice system and then continue to do so? They are real issues in justice administration. Wounded justice can be of three kinds—

(1) That the policemen/officers are wholly responsible

(2) That the policemen/officers are partly responsible

(3) That the policemen/officers are not responsible

In other words, police bring wounded justice upon others; others bring it upon people; forces of nature bring it upon people. What to do and how to go about it? This is the real problem. In cases where the police is fully responsible, the police must change and it only can bring the desired changes. In cases the police are partly responsible, the police can do a lot to put down the evils in administration of justice. If they do thus far, then a lot of changes can be seen in the area of justice administration. There are international laws enacted and passed for administration of just justice and the police can enforce such laws to avoid *wounded justice* administration. Policeman as individuals may be very good people, but they become bad, as the allegation goes, when they wear the uniform and become a part of the uniformed strength. Psychologists say that they become emotional when they are in a group and are rational when they are alone. Group-mind of the police is different from the individual mind. Benedict Spinoza's (1632-1677) friend was imprisoned for expressing his ideas and was brutally treated that he died within a year. Likewise, a number of cases may be seen down the centuries and in all such instances, it is not individual policeman who behaves. It is the group mind that works as the killer in police work.

Wounded Justice and Just Justice

Some policemen/officers argue that there is nothing called wounded justice - or - just justice. What is seen or to be seen is justice and nothing more or nothing less. According to them, justice is relative and as such what seems to police as just may look like "wounded justice or injustice" to the suspect. Interpretations make something just or unjust as the case may be. Critics to this view advance the argument that the interpretations of something as good or bad depends upon the character and an upright conscience of the interpreter. A just policeman/officer is one who possesses a mature, dispassionate, disciplined, moral and an upright conscience. How many in police service have such a conscience?

Can a policeman/officer administer justice in a mature, dispassionate, disciplined way with an upright conscience in the existing socio-political situation? Studies show that it is not possible to do so in the ordinary circumstances? Why? One reason is that the politicians have a say in the administration of justice by police. Policemen/officers can not, as a rule, escape from the clutches of politicians in Indian democracy. The police, more often than not, can not act in accordance with their reason and justness in action. The policeman/officer is not a free man in the present political set-up. He is correctly described as a slave to politicians and in some cases, to the whims of politicians. Wounded justice may be the outcome in such situations. Spinoza in his philosophy of scientific rationalism said: "A free man is one who lives according to the dictates of reason alone; he is not led by fear but directly desires what is good". Today, the allegation is that many a policeman/officer is lead by the fear of politicians and precisely therefore, he can administer only wounded justice.

10

Wounded Justice and Committee on Police Reforms: Looking Ahead

"Despite its shortcomings, the Indian police have performed a reasonable job in the past years. What are the strength of Indian police as it is organized today?" - this is the second question seen in the questionnaire prepared by the Committee on Police Reforms appointed by Government of India in 2000. The strengths are many and that is the precise reason why the service is retained even today. The people spend nearly or more than nine thousand crores of rupees for maintaining Indian police and it is not a small amount. But, they expect justice from the service and wounded justice administration has no scope. The Committee, therefore, asks further: "What are the major weakness of Indian police as you perceive?" This is a too generalized question that can not be answered in three or four sentences or in two or three paragraphs. The system did not or could not rise up to the expectation of the people and certainly, the people want to reform the system. That is the precise reason why the Committee on Police Reforms was appointed at a national level. The decision to appoint a Committee engenders a ceaseless striving, a restless longing of the people of India to have a police system that ensures justice to the people. If the people get what they want, if their desires are fulfilled, then they will be happy. Darwin's concept of evolution and later theories of evolution to the Omega together with Bismarck's will to power - all these approaches and thoughts make the people and society to take steps for creating a better world. Defects and failures are there in life, but from failures and defeats, people get the will to power and out of such defects, defeats and failures, people get new strength and greatness. The Committee, for example, thinks that "there is a growing body of opinion that more women in a police force would have a humanizing and sobering effect on the force as a whole. What is your opinion about increasing the percentage of women in police?" The Committee wants to humanize the police and then how? It uses the words "police force" and the question is how to humanize a force?" If the failure of the police in Indian democracy has been due to their reluctance to accept the police as a service (instead of as a force), then the repeated use of the word 'force' in the questionnaire does not mean much for the reformers of police. 'Humanizing' is a word that means a lot. Does it mean that the police is not human? If it is not human, then what is it? This needs an answer before we proceed further. The Committee wants to see some sobering effect brought on the 'police force' as a whole. Again what is meant by 'sobering?' 'Humanize' means '*to make* humane, kind or gentle' and 'sobering' means (among other meanings) 'showing self control'. In both expressions, one finds an element of 'wounded justice'. 'Humanizing' is marked by a greater sensitiveness to the social well being of the people and the police can do so in very many ways. For this, the police must have 'self-control' (sobering). How far can the entry of women to police service ensure the humanizing and sobering effect on the police is not the question that is answered here. Police can be humanized only through socialization and inculcation of human values and human rights principles. They can be sober only if they develop ego strengths. This can be obtained by being and becoming ethical in life and behaviour. The police must have an ideal which has a basis on morality and legality. One can not exist without the other or if at all one exists without the other, then its existence will be short lived. Aristotle writes: "We are just, temperate, courageous, and the like from our very birth, natural moral states exist even in children and lower animals.... It is neither by nature nor in defiance of nature that virtues arise in us. Nature gives us the capacity is perfected by habit". How can the policeman's capacity to be sober be developed.?

Cultured, People Friendly Police Service

The recommendations of the National Police Commission are kept in abeyance - or better not accepted by the democratic governments that came into power from time to time. Hence a Committee on Police Reforms is constituted to guide the police service in the 21st century. The Committee asks: "How can we give Indian police an image of a cultured, people friendly police *force* without sacrificing the effectiveness of police?" The question presupposes that the police today is not cultured and people friendly. In other words, the police administers wounded justice to people. 'Police force' in dictionary means "any body of persons combined for joint action" and the police in a democracy is more than that. Its functions are not limited to joint action alone and if it means only joint action, then making it cultured or people friendly ceases to have much meaning and relevance. Fundamentally and ultimately, the police in a democracy is a service – a public facility and the recommendations must be made keeping in view such perspectives and perceptions of the police service. Police have inherited a culture from the British past and the culture has been partly responsible for keeping police away from the people. This may be the reason why the Committee wants to get the considered views to the question: "How do you think the existing gap between the public expectations and police performance can be bridged?" No doubt, there exists a gap between the police and the people and the reasons for the gap must be identified. One of the major reasons is the administration of wounded justice by the police in the existing situation. British policization of Indian police could not socialize the police. The failure or reluctance of the administration in democracy to socialize the police added further complications and they could not become people friendly. Half hearted attempts were made here and there in the recent past, but they too did not yield the desired effect. As a result, there arose a growing demand to humanize and socialize the police service. A new culture had to be developed - a culture that promoted people friendly attitude and approach. Police ethics - that becomes a matter of serious thought in police-citizen interactions. Cultured behaviour means nothing but behaving according to the laws - social and cultural - of a society. The penal codes and procedural codes do not teach about how to behave. It is the cultural, social and moral codes that teach everyone to behave in a cultured manner. It being so, the policemen need to be inculcated with the finer points in human behaviour by exposing them to the social, cultural and moral codes of behaviour. "Never use epithets to a man in police custody"– this is not said in the penal, procedural laws. It is given in the written/unwritten social, moral and cultural codes. Guide police behaviour by social, moral and cultural codes. The passions of hatred, overenthusiasm, vindictiveness, vengeance, retribution, wounded justice, anger, envy follow from the lack of proper socialization and super-ego formation in policemen. I have seen many policemen/officers behaving in an uncultured way and most of them come from a background which did not or could not provide adequate facilities for proper socialization and super-ego development. I have seen that much of police learning of behavior takes place when they are on the job. Police want social approval of what they do, but they do not get it. Why? Policeman's working environment becomes as important and as natural a factor in the development of culture as is the physical environment in the growth of the biological organism at an early stage. The first few years of one's service have very decisive influence on a policeman's later behaviour.

The working environment and social interaction during the early years of policemen's service shape their lives. Hence, one of the ways to make cultured policemen is to control the environment in which they act and hence think and feel. In police training colleges, they can be taught more about human behaviour, but this direct education has limited influence on their behaviour unless they are provided with facilitating environments for further development. The working environment has a decisive influence on their development of culture. This, unfortunately, is an insight which the police hierarchy had hitherto not recognized. They express difficulty to recognize this truth and even greater difficulty in putting into practice. It is the responsibility of the police hierarchy to create a kind of environment in which desirable growth, culture and development will take place. In such an environment, people friendly police becomes a reality.

Weaker Sections and Women

Committee on Police Reforms asks: "Police handling of weaker sections and women have been coming under constant flack from all quarters. What steps can be taken to improve police behaviour to the weaker sections and women?" The terms 'weaker sections' as academically defined, socially described or caste-wise treated may mean nothing when they are dealt with by police. Anybody, irrespective of their birth, caste, social or economic position, who is defenseless and helpless before the police has to be treated as one belonging to the weaker sections of the society. In that sense, any person who becomes a victim of abuse of power or misuse of authority is a member of the weaker sections as far as the police are concerned. In that sense, anybody who is not influential with the police is a member of the weaker sections. In that sense, anybody who becomes a victim of police misbehaviour or administration of wounded justice is a member of the weaker sections. Perhaps, complaints against police from people who belong to the section of the society which is not traditionally and academically considered as "weaker" may be more than those who are socially, economically or Constitutionally treated as "weaker" in Indian society. Perhaps, the number of people who dies in police custody or subjected to torture, harassment, coercion etc. by police may be more from the section of the society which is not presently treated as "weaker" in India. Whatever that be, the Committee is candid enough to admit that police handling of weaker sections of the society is far away from being satisfactory and it needs to improve police behaviour to the weaker sections.

The fundamental question is: "why don't the police treat man as man in their interactions with them?" Human rights activists may uphold man and his worth as the supreme value. But, some police officers fail to or refuse to internalize this value of human existence. A man has a human *essence* basides and beyond his community of birth or status he enjoys. Police job had meaning only when it ensures justice to people. Police life is nothing until its benefits are extended to people without any discrimination to caste, colour, creed and community. A policeman/officer can make sense of his life only if he refuses to administer wounded justice. For this, he must be told about the meaning of '*I-Thou personal relationship*' and the *"we" approach* in police work. Such a relationship and an approach will strengthen police human relationship. The police must make all attempts to have a conscious will and commitment to an atmosphere in which there is a much deeper awareness of the community they serve. I quote Baber, an existentialist philosopher here: "for only men who are capable of truly saying *thou* to one *another* can truly say *we* with one another". He continues: "A man is truly saved from the one not by separation but only by being bound up in genuine communion". If the policemen can have this vision in life, his behaviour to all people in society will be praiseworthy.

Women are increasingly coming to police stations as petitioners, complainants, witnesses, suspects, arrestees and so on. The police behaviour with women becomes a topic of discussion among the people owing to several reasons. No doubt, still there is resistance in many women to come to police. There are a number of laws, rules and departmental circulars specifying how must be the nature of police behaviour towards them. Yet, complaints are heard. Police is a man dominated organization and in such a set-up, women may feel uncomfortable to be amidst men, A woman in a police station may become a new experience for some. But, a well disciplined policeman/officer must look at her only as a witness, complainant, suspect, arrestee and so on as the case may be. She is not and must not become an object of pleasure for anybody. This attitude towards women may work better than the laws and departmental circulars controlling police-women interaction. Policemen ought to become more responsible - more fully human than they otherwise be whenever they interact with women, in uniform. They must remember that we are living in a world of women's liberation movement and precisely therefore, the women's voice will be heard more loudly than that of men and policemen.

Public Trust and Cooperation

"Today, police do not enjoy public trust and cooperation to the extent similar organizations do in developed countries. How do we remedy this?" - asks the Committee on Police Reforms. The fact that the police in developed countries enjoy better trust than what the police in India have indicates that wounded justice administration may be less in those countries. In a democracy, police can get public trust only if they prove that they can be trusted. But, whenever they show weakness, lack of integrity, disrespect to administer fair justice, partiality, parochialism, susceptibility to political influence, corruption and corrupt practices, unholy *nexus* with undesirables or underworld criminals etc., necessarily they lose public trust. People watch, they evaluate and then decide. The trust is lost over a period and what is required is a holistic treatment. To quote the National Human Rights Commission: "In recent years, there has been growing concern in the country that the processes of governance have, on occasion, been eroded by a *nexus* between criminals, less than scrupulous political elements and members of the executive lacking in integrity. The deleterious effects on human rights resulting from such a *nexus* can be gauged from the nature of the petitions received by this Commission, many of which complain of violations because the supposed protectors of rights have themselves turned predators. It is because of such complaints that the Commission felt compelled to call for systematic reforms in the police, designed to insulate its investigation work from extraneous influences that would otherwise destroy its integrity".

Public trust can be established only if :-

(1) the conviction rate is increased and fair justice administration is ensured,

(2) people friendly attitude and approach are shown making the people to understand that the police are the people and the people are the police,

(3) scientific methods are applied and psychological techniques are resorted to during interviewing witnesses, interrogating suspects, collecting intelligence and promoting community policing etc.

True policing is built on restraint and control of instincts in police work. When people see custodial torture, rape and death in police stations, how can they trust the police? The

Supreme Court of India in Kishore Sing Vs. State of Rajasthan (AIR 1982 SC 625) held the view that "nothing is more cowardly and unconscionable than a person in police custody being beaten up and nothing inflicts a deeper wound on our Constitutional rights". Public trust is not something that can be created just like that over a night, too soon. It requires several years' hard work and committed endeavours from all members in police service to make an attitudinal change among the people. The public trust thus created may be destroyed by a few custodial tortures, rapes, murders or administration of wounded justice or use of indecent expressions and epithets or by corruption or by unholy *nexus* with politicians, business men, underworld criminals etc. seen, heard or reported in the media from here and there in the Country. The British brought a police system and the democratic governments allowed the system to continue and the public have lost their trust on the system. Nevertheless, the need is that India deserves a police service which is of highest integrity, quality, dependability and commanding public trust and appreciation. It needs public cooperation and willing participation. Community policing is a good concept which has been successfully implemented in many developed countries. India too may follow it. In some States, the vested interests dilute the concept of community policing to suit to their political interests. They call it then 'popular policing or people's policing' and the intention is different from what it is in community policing. After India became independent till date, the police have been misused for obtaining political mileage and for serving the self interests of the powerful, the affluent and the influential. Public trust thus was lost and public cooperation thus was not ensured. The Committee on Police Reforms now want to establish public trust and their cooperation with police. The Committee itself admits --

(1) The quality and technology of investigation of criminal cases needs be upgraded;

(2) Police are not well equipped to deal with crimes which are committed by using sophisticated methodology.

(3) The current rates of conviction are very poor and if these areas identified by the Committee are corrected, certainly the people may come forward with their cooperation and participation.

Police Attitude and Wounded Justice Administration

The formation of attitude is of paramount interest in police community interactions. Recruitment of candidates possessing an upright conscience and an appropriate attitude assumes importance. Perhaps, administration of well developed aptitude and attitude tests at the time of recruitment may help to a great extent to find our suitable candidates to police service. At present, the eligibility is tested and suitability is not. At the level of constabulary, at present, no such test is conducted. The qualification of police constables is a pass in S.S.L.C. examination. As crimes are becoming more complex and complicated, it becomes necessary that even police constables may be entrusted with handling of sophisticated crimes and criminals. As the general educational standards of the public have gone up, there is a school of thought which adheres to the view that there must be better qualified constables to do crime work. In some foreign countries, there are graduate constables who are entrusted with crime work. A rise in the educational qualification of the constables can, certainly, enhance public trust on police and correspondingly the public appreciation for police work. Today, the people have a feeling, well founded or not, that moderately educated constables damage investigation and cause wounded justice administration. Sub-inspectors are degree holders and precisely therefore people insist that they alone must investigate crimes. Often it so happens that they get little or no time to do everything connected with crime investigation. Necessarily, the work load of sub-inspectors compels them to entrust certain jobs connected with investigation of crimes to police constables who, according to the public, are unqualified or ill-qualified. This feeling can be eradicated if better qualified constables come to the scene. The Committee on Police Reforms, it seems, is convinced of this fact and therefore, it wants to collect the view from the respondents to their questionnaire to a proposal whether or not the recruitment agency must evaluate the aptitude, comprehension and general knowledge of the constables. Certainly the proposal is a welcome step to ensure better quality and to eliminate wounded justice administration during the investigation of crimes. All said and done, the Committee is, it seems, worried about corrupt practices during the recruitment processes. If corruption creeps into, then there is very chance to get the undesirable candidates enlisted and consequently all the defects connected with wounded justice administration multiplied.

A sub-inspector is the kin-pin in a police station and therefore the recruitment of suitable candidates is a *conditio sine qua non* for obtaining public confidence, appreciation, cooperation and participation in police work. Young blood with commitment, values, religious zeal and missionary enthusiasm must come in large numbers to ensure public trust and cooperation.

The Committee on Police Reforms wants to know the specific kind of attitudes and behaviour that must be seen among the policemen. The functions of police, as the people describe them, are oriented to administer just justice. Police is a man-oriented service which must improve human life. Every policeman must essentially be a humanist. The legal ideal is not something artificial or arbitary imposed upon anyone who is at heart antagonistic to it. Every legal ideal has a social basis and everything social has a legal development. It being so, the personality traits of a policeman - the director general of police included - must have these sublime ideals. One can not force a man to be good, legal, social and decent. The goodness must come from within. Goodness in police work and legality in police action are not opposed to each other. They are mutually dependent. I think that the police life must have (1) honour and dignity; (2) legality and morality; (3) equity, good conscience and justice. In all, one must see that human service is the aim of police work.

Police Training and Wounded Justice

"Do you think that the present system is suitable for a community friendly, service oriented law enforcement agency? If not, what is wrong?" - the Committee on Police Reforms asks. The question is not relevant as the question contains the answer too. The training can not be and is not suitable for community friendly, service oriented law enforcement. If it were so, then there would not have been so much and, so many criticisms against the police in India. The British system of police training essentially continues even now although some half-hearted attempts were reluctantly made here and there to implement the recommendations of the Central Committee on Police Training. The Committee wanted to give a new orientation to police training, but owing to the lack of political and administrative will, the implementation of the Committee's recommendations has been frustratingly slow. No change in attitude - in approach - in outlook comes into being. Tragically enough, a man becomes a policeman after his training and the policeman means the *policeman* as described and shown in films, TV serials, fictions and news paper reports.

A lot has been said and written about modernizing police training. But, they are just empty words and hollow utterances. I therefore do not want to write more about improving police training as I myself have written a number of articles on the subject. It is not the lack of knowledge about the subject that police training is not improved, rather it is due to the low priority given to training that the training is neglected. The Committee on Police Reforms just asks this question and the intentions are at best suspicious. The Committee knows the answers too. The whole philosophy and outlook of police training, there is a view, are based on a degenerated concept of '*muscle rules or can rule*' the people in a democracy. It may be the reason why the Committee asks: "Do you think the present system of outdoor training serves a useful purpose? Do you think there is scope for modification in the present outdoor training? Explain". I have noticed that most of the trainees who undergo strenuous outdoor training just forget about it when they go out of the training institutions. They refuse to do so and that is enough to argue that the present system of outdoor training serves no useful purpose. Just like the old folk-lore dances, country-side performances etc. are retained by the people for the new generations to see how the old generation of people developed their talents through art, culture and dances, the present police administration retains the dilapidated, degenerated and useless outdoor training today. For example, lathy drill and mob-operation techniques are items of curiosity and they can never be of any use in a democracy. The cuts and jabs are human right violations and bayonet training is an atrocity on human life and dignity. Yet, they are taught in some police training institutions! The teachers and the taught do not know the purpose behind and most interestingly the British who introduced bayonet training laugh at the Indian police when they see the bayonet training taught to the civil police in India democracy. The bayonet training now for civil police in India is an item of news value for the British press. This I say because the Central Committee on Police Training, as early as in 1973, recommended abolition of bayonet training for civil police in India. Yet, there are police training institutions now offering bayonet training. What a surprise indeed!

'Well begun is half done' - if that is a truth, training assumes a lot of importance in administration of justice and in administration of wounded justice as well. "Life has meaning"– every police trainer must feel so with Browning and so does the police life. This must go deep into every trainee when he undergoes his course in the campus. To quote Will Durant: "so much of our life is meaningless, a self-canceling vacillation and futility; we strive with the chaos about us and within; but we would believe all the while that there is something vital and significant in us, could we but decipher our own souls". Every policeman wants to understand: "the life means for us constantly to transform into light and flame all what we are or meet with"- says Nietzsche in 'The Joyful Wisdom', If this is the philosophy of life, the training must be oriented to inculcate this value in all. The police life means for all to transform into light and flame all that the policemen/officers are or to meet with light and flame means justice, goodness, equity and good conscience. One doubts very much whether or not the police trainers had this thought in their mind as someone very humorously puts it: '*some police trainers had all sorts of wisdom except common sense - the common sense in a democratic set up*'.

Police Station and Wounded Justice

Once a superintendent of police wrote in his inspection report that "the police station is stenching just as the officers and men are with their corruption and malpractices". Yet, the human content in police stations decides the nature of service rendered. The Committee on Police Reforms limits its questions on police stations in three and the first one is: "Do you think the present police stations are well equipped to tackle the problems of the near future? What changes would you envisage?" The question is vague as no one is clear about the problems of the neat feature. Problems are many and the major problem is the human content inside. Most of the police stations are housed in old and dilapidated buildings with no furniture and facilities. Police stations have no suicide proof custodial facility, rather have the old lockups with heavy locks and doors with bars. People commit suicide inside the lockups and if at all police stations are provided with latest furniture, reception counters, visitors' rooms, drinking water etc., they may not serve any useful purpose if the human content is lacking human qualities. "How should be the appearance of a police stations?"– the Committee asks. If the *poojaries* (the priests) are not nice people, then the devotees to the temple may not get the '*prasadem*'. Just like that, one can make the police stations in the shape of a temple, mosque, gurudwara or church but the priests inside must possess human qualities and people friendly attitudes. They ensure just justice. People refer human behaviour to penal and procedural laws being applied in police stations. Vehicles, phones, computers, wireless sets, weapons, scientific aids to investigation etc. offer utility in police work, but human behaviour gives beauty to the work done. People friendly approaches take the policemen/officers directly to a particular person and that makes the police work praiseworthy.

"Do you think the present police set up at the station level inspires confidence in the public, especially the socially disadvantaged? Do you have to improve the situation?" - puts the Committee in its questionnaire. Again the question is not clear. Of what 'set-up' the Committee is speaking? Does it mean the administrative set up? Does it mean the functional set up? Whatever may be the set up, people want justice from the police. Whatever may be the set up, the '*behavioural set up*' matters a lot to the common man. How do the personnel in police stations receive the petitioners, complainants, witnesses, suspects, arrestees, visitors and so on tells about the worth and value of police set up. The manner in which a service is rendered, a service is delayed, a service is denied and a service is refused make the service enviable or not–more than what service is extended to the man on the street. People condemn the discourtesy and appreciate any good gesture. Policemen/officers working in police stations - at the cutting edge level - make the stations a hell or a heaven. They can blame no one else - no outside circumstances - no outside agencies - no political interferences responsible for misbehaviour. Police behaviour at police stations must be marked by greater sensitiveness to people's need and welfare. Police is to serve and protect; police is the friend in need; police is for all, but belongs to none. These are and must be the basic features of the 'behavioural set up' in police administration.

What must be the facilities for the public who approach police stations? - the Committee wants to elicit information on that. The answer to the question is that the people must get an 'emotional first aid' in all police stations. They must feel that they have come to the 'right place' for help and for this they must get a treatment showing that they are *invitees* to police stations. A police station is a public facility and people must feel so. The principles of behaviour which the policemen apply in police stations/in their job must not be opposite to those which people practice in their lives. A police sub-culture shows certain behavioural patterns which the dominant culture in society does not accept. This creates the problem in police-citizen interaction.

If at all no physical pleasure giving facilities are provided in police stations, people want them to be recognized as human beings with dignity. For example, once a detinue in a police lock up told me that he had a hell of a time in a police station. The police station was housed in an old building. It had a cemented floor and a policeman poured water on the floor so much so that he could not sit or sleep. True or false is allegation against the police, one does not like to hear such allegations. There come news reports, sometimes about and against the police which disturb human conscience. The blinding episode, custodial rape, custodial murder etc. indicate how atrocious are some of the policemen. Whatever may be the facilities provided to the general public in a police station and if they are misused for committing human rights violations on people, the facilities given in police stations cease to have any meaning to anybody; rather become a supreme dishonour to human dignity and democratic values.

Human Rights and Wounded Justice

Just two questions in the questionnaire and that is all about human rights! - Why so? The first question is : "It is said that 60 per cent of the arrests made by police in the country are really unnecessary. This is in addition to the totally unauthorized detention in the police stations, which are not even recorded. An unnecessary arrest becomes the starting point for further human rights violations, like beating up in lockup etc. What steps do you think need to be taken to eliminate unnecessary arrests? The question relates to unnecessary arrests and unauthorized detentions in police custody. The answer needs to be to the former and therefore the answer is simple. The Supreme Court of India, in D.K. Basu Vs. State of West Bengal (Writ Petition CRL No. 539 of 1986) has clearly given some directives to police for observing them at the time of arrests. Certainly it will protect the human rights of people and will eliminate the abuse of power/misuse of authority by police.

More important is to identify the areas of police violations of human rights. A casual reading of the Reports of the National Human Rights Commission may show the many and various areas of human rights violations by police. Some reported cases of human rights violations by police as given in the 1996-97 report of the National Human Rights Commission have been given in Chapter 1 of this book. They show that human rights violations are seen -

(1) Death in alleged fake encounters;

(2) Police encounter killings;

(3) Custodial murder/death

(4) Attempt at rape

(5) Police torture

(6) Misbehavior and torture by police

(7) Mass cremation of unidentified dead bodies etc.

Besides, there can be many other areas of police violations of human rights from unnecessary handcuffing to many other cruel and degrading treatment. Any human rights violation tantamounts to wounded justice administration. "An unnecessary arrest becomes the starting point for further human rights violations" - the Committee observes. The real causes of human rights violations are to be found in the violators themselves. 'The police nature' when one wears a police uniform has, I think, a biological basis more than the moral, legal, social, psychological and human rights basis. It is not a legal man who behaves when one violates human rights. It is the biological organism - the emotional man - the man with instincts behaves. The human rights violators need to have a mental therapy. A human rights friendly policeman will introspect and seek to understand the cause of his emotions and instinctual behavior. There may be even unconscious drives which make one to behave in a particular way. Sigmund Freud had maintained that any frustration in the expression of man's unconscious drives might manifest itself in some painful disturbance in his conscious life. I have interviewed some human rights unfriendly policemen/officers and have convinced myself about the influence of unconscious drives on their human rights unfriendly behaviour. Police departments all over the Country have many experts in many fields, but rarely I have seen psychologists/clinical psychologists/psychotherapists working to extend their services to problem officials. Some policemen/officers have mental health problems and may be suffering from personality disorders. They cause human rights violations and they can be helped by offering counseling or by other psychotherapy. A human right unfriendly behaviour is an irrational behaviour and the irrational motives lose their force when a human rights unfriendly policeman/officer understands where exactly lies the problem and he can do so by the help of a psychotherapist/clinical psychologist.

It is the National Police Commission which pointed out the fact that 60 per cent of the arrests made by the police in India was either unnecessary or unjustified and if that was the truth, it showed the extent of wounded justice administration. Police behaviours prior to, during and immediately after the arrests are of great significance. Policemen have an authoritarian ego and they speak with authority which may be resented against or reacted by the people. This may be followed by heated exchanges. In one case, I was told that the sub-inspector while he patrolled his jurisdiction found a man shouting at another. The sub-inspector asked him to get into his jeep and he refused. He asked "why?" and the police officer was not prepared to answer. He was told that an answer to his question - why he was told to get into the jeep - would be given to him when he reached the police station. Of course, to know the grounds of arrest was a fundamental right to a citizen, but his questioning the sub-inspector did hurt his authoritarian ego. On reaching the police station, the answer was given by the muscles of the police officer which ultimately ended in the death of that man. A case was registered against the guilty police officer and later he was convicted for life.

Human rights are, I repeat, concepts of recent origin in India and precisely therefore many a policeman does not know the full extent and application of human rights concepts in police work. The National Human Rights Commission initiates many steps for the training and retraining of police personnel so as to make them more aware of and sensitive to human rights considerations in police work. Many police training institutions are undertaking special courses on human rights to police personnel. In some of the courses I have offered faculty assistance, many policemen/officers have asked me a variety of doubts for clarification. They asked me whether or not "this" amounted to human rights violation - "that" amounted to human rights violation. There were many doubts in them and therefore I thought that they ought to be taught the various types of human rights violations which are besides and beyond the *'informal arrests'* and 'illegal detention' in police custody. The questionnaire, however, keeps silence on such aspects as it seeks only views relating to various steps the Committee may recommended to eliminate unnecessary arrests. Whatever that be, there is a view that the recommendations may concentrate more on the behaviour of police personnel prior to, during and after the arrests of the people. After creating a full and thorough awareness of human rights, let every policeman list out various areas of human rights violations in police work. He must be honest to himself, his soul and people and certainly it will help to eliminate not only unnecessary arrests, but also many other human rights violations about which nothing has been mentioned in the questionnaire prepared by the Committee.

The Committee on Reforms asks further: "Another major reason for people feeling harassed by the police is the non-registration of crimes when people approach the police station. What suggestions you have to see that the malady is rectified?" The use of the word's "harassment", "malady" etc. is indicative of the reality that there exists wounded justice administration today. Some respondents to the questionnaire are skeptic about the relationship between non-registration of crimes and human rights violations. Nevertheless, when a high powered Committee puts it under the sub-title Human Rights in the questionnaire, they search for suggestions to rectify the "malady" if it exists. One suggestion which, I think, may work out is to apply the principles of victimological compensation to the victims of abuse of power/misuse of authority. The compensation thus awarded must be realized from the officer responsible for the same. Of course, there are provisions existing in the present Code of Criminal Procedure-1973 to deal with such situations. The Committee now has raised the issue in the questionnaire and it means that the evil persists in spite of the provisions in law. More than the legal aspects, human rights activists are concerned with the behavioural aspects of the police functionaries when they refuse a service to the citizens. The Committee asks: "What steps do you suggest to bring about a change in the attitude, mind set and behaviour of individual policeman, the group behaviour of the police and the behaviour of police as a 'Force'?

Accountability and Wounded Justice

"What mechanisms are necessary to ensure that the police perform their legitimate duties without the fear of uncalled for interference from outside, at the same time, ensuring accountability of the police for their acts of commission and omission?" - asks the Committee. Again: "How do we insulate police at various levels from undue political interference without taking away its accountability?" These two questions pose serious issues relating to justice/wounded justice administration. What are the uncalled for interference from outside police performance adversely? What is meant by the accountability of police? - to whom? What is meant by undue political interference? Is there something called due political interference? Where do the politicians interfere? Why do they interfere? The Committee speaks of the uncalled for interference! Does it mean that there is something known as "called for interference" from outside? What is meant by outside? And why do they interfere? Do the police ensure fair justice without interference from outside? What were the circumstances which created a situation in police for entertaining *uncalled for interference* in police work? How can they be called uncalled for? During the British rule, the police performed their job without political interference and did the police administer fair justice to the people? Researches showed that they did not or they could not. Why? Might be that they were behaving as the weapon of the then British government. What about the situation in the democratic set up? Are the police behaving as the weapon of the political party in power? What the British Government did in the past are followed by the political parties in Government now. Perhaps a Police Act which was framed in that perspective could help the politicians and the government in power to continue what the British did. This necessitates the enacting of a new Police Act for Indian Police. It seems that the Committee on Police Reforms is very much concerned with the elimination of wounded justice administration by Indian police from its inception in 1861. People have a lot of hopes on the Committee's recommendations for creating a new culture in police service. Will that hope be actualized during the years to come or will the story of police continue as it has been till now?

Appendix

Committee on Police Reforms, Government of India, Ministry of Home Affairs

QUESTIONNAIRE

General

(1) Keeping in view the revolution in information technology, globalization and liberalization of economy as well as the emerging new socio-political scenario, like more autonomy for Panchayats and Muncipalities, urbanization, political fragmentation, organized crime, etc what according to you are the five most important challenges facing the Indian police in the near future. State briefly according to importance

(2) Despite its shortcomings, the Indian police have performed a reasonable job in the past years. What are the strengths of Indian police as it is organized today?

1

2

3

4

5

(3) What are the major weaknesses of Indian police as you perceive?

1

2

3

4

5

(4) What are the various pieces of legislation in your State governing the working of the police?

(5) Do you have separate Acts regarding civil police and State Armed Police. If so, do you think separate Acts are necessary? Does your State have any other specialized police force like Commando force, Coast Guard, Special Security Force etc. Please give details.

Personnel Management

(6) At the police Headquarters is there a proper arrangement for manpower planning based on realistic forecasts and a good career planning (personnel management)? What improvements do you suggest to attend to this?

(7) Promotional prospects of subordinate ranks in most States are poor due to poor career planning and ad hoc measures for promotions and recruitment. Is this true about your State? It so what remedial measures do you suggest?

(8) What is the machinery to redress the grievances of the police personnel? Are you satisfied with it? The National Police Commission has made certain suggestions in this regard. Have they been implemented? If not, what are your suggestions?

(9) There is a growing body of opinion that more women in a police force would have a humanizing and sobering

effect on the force as a whole. What is your opinion about increasing the percentage of women in police?

(10) There is a feeling that there is too much permissiveness in the conduct of policemen, especially in the officers' rank, and that the Conduct Rules and "Code of Conduct" are not being enforced with any determination.

What are your suggestions in this regard?

(11) In the Defence Services there is a practice of retiring personnel at various levels, who are unable to get promotion or required specialization after a certain number of years-say 15 years etc. This promotes efficiency, motivation and high morale. Would you support a similar system of screening of personnel irrespective of rank in the police. If such a system is adopted, there has to be simultaneously a scheme of rehabilitation for such personnel who are weeded out. In case you do not agree with the above, what system would you like to have, to take care of such persons who have lost their professional usefulness.

Control of Police, Transfers, Accountability

(12) Are there any jobs currently performed by police which can be privatized?

(13) Are there any duties currently performed by police which can be divested without affecting the effectiveness of police? List them.

(14) The service conditions, like extended hours of duty, lack of adequate housing, etc., play a great role in influencing the police behaviour.

What steps do you propose to improve the morale of the policeman and the force?

(15) There is an argument that the police has taken upon itself willingly or otherwise a number of duties which should not strictly be within the purview of police duties. Some people feel that these extra duties like offences under the Excise Act, offences under various local and special Acts especially those relating to social legislation, and duties like service of summons, escorting of prisoners, verification of passport etc. removal of encroachments, electricity thefts, should be shed so that police can concentrate on the IPC crime and certain other core functions? Others feel that since most of these have a direct or indirect bearing on law and order or crime, police can ill afford to shed these functions. In fact they go to extent of saying that police should become a service organization and also take up counselling activities. What are your views in this regard?

(16) In the above context the police have in metropolitan areas, taken over a very large number of activities like licensing of eating houses, licensing of places of entertainment and amusement, licensing cinema halls, hotels, guest houses, massage parlors, swimming pools, placement of hoarding for advertisement etc. Do you think these functions rightfully belong to the police department?

Public Interface

(17) How can we give Indian police an image of a cultured, people friendly police force without sacrificing the effectiveness of police?

(18) How do you think the existing gap between the public expectations and police performance can be bridged?

(19) What is the mechanism for redressal of public grievances in your State?

(20) Is the mechanism able to effectively redress public grievance? Have the recommendations of NPC in this

regard been implemented? If not what mechanism would you suggest?

(21) Police handling of weaker sections and women have been coming under constant flack from all quarters. What steps can be taken to improve police behaviour to the weaker sections and women?

(22) Do you think that there should be a "Police Complaints Authority" either statutory or otherwise, to attend to public complaints against police atrocities?

(23) Today police do not enjoy public trust and cooperation to the extent similar organizations do in developed countries. How do we remedy this?

(24) Do you think an effective beat patrol system will contribute to the improved public perception and cooperation and control of crime? What can be done to revamp the beat system?

Policing-operational Aspect

(25) What steps need be taken to upgrade the quality and technology of investigation of criminal cases?

(26) Criminals are using increasingly sophisticated methodology and are harnessing the latest technology for committing crime. The nature of crime too has witnessed a shift in the recent past. At present police does not seem to be well equipped to deal with this phenomena. What steps do you suggest?

(27) The current rates of conviction are very low. What do you think are the reasons for this low rates of conviction:

1

2

3

4

(28) What steps can be taken to remedy this trend?

(29) Traffic management is assuming new importance in view of the high rates of accidents and losses on the roads. What can be done to improve traffic management? What can be done to improve coordination with various bodies like Municipal, PWD, authorities and with public utility agencies; what can be done to improve police-road user relations?

(30) A recommendation made by many Committees is that there should be a vertical separation of investigation functions from law and order duties. What is your view on this? Is there any partial or total separation of these functions in your State?

(31) Do you have a highway patrol/policing system in your State? Do you need it? Is there any plan for setting up a proper highway policing set up in your State? Please elaborate.

(32) What steps do you suggest to improve the working of Government Railway Police, especially in the context of explosives etc. being carried in trains, and terrorists targeting trains?

(33) Indian police is designed predominantly for rural policing. What changes in the basic unit would you suggest for policing a city? Do you think that there is a case for transferring some of the police powers (example: as regards public nuisances, etc.) to Municipalities and metropolitan authorities.

(34) What is the system of village policing you have? Is village police as a separate entity, necessary, and effective and how are village police personnel compensated? Do you have any suggestions to improve the system?

(35) Are any police functions being performed on a regular basis by the Home Guards? If so what functions? Are

they given armed duties? How frequently or over what period (months etc.) are they used in a year?

Weapons and Equipment

(36) Are you satisfied with the weapons used by the civil police, armed police and specialized forces at present? What changes would you like to see? What about adequacy of ammunition?

(37) Are you satisfied with the training and annual musketry practice, and the proficiency tests; what improvements do you suggest?

(38) There is a feeling that in India all policemen are superficially trained in the use of weapons. As a result few are adept in the use of arms. In some countries, only selected personnel with an aptitude for handling fire arms are trained but they are very well trained. Do you think this system is better than the Indian system or do you think Indian system is adequate? What improvements would you suggest?

(39) What improvements in the communication machinery of police would you like to see?

(40) How do we improve the mobility of Indian police keeping in view the budgetary constraints?

Intelligence

(41) What is the intelligence gathering set-up in your State?

(42) Are you satisfied with coordination with other intelligence gathering agencies including the IB? Is the sharing of information satisfactory and timely? If not your suggestions please.

(43) What improvement do you suggest in the organization and working of the Union Government agencies so that

they could render better support in terms of crime data, supply of criminal intelligence, forensic science inputs, professional training, fingerprinting, etc.?

(44) How do you improve its effectiveness and how do you ensure more accurate and faster dissemination to the appropriate levels?

Federal Crimes

(45) There is a growing demand for treating certain crimes like terrorism, kidnapping, arms trafficking, hijacking, counterfeiting, certain other offences against the State and other crimes having a nation wide ramification, as federal crimes, the enforcement of which should be put exclusively in the hands of central law enforcement agencies like the CBI or a new Body to be created. What is your opinion about this? What crimes should it be treated as federal crimes?

(46) If you feel that the Central Government agency would not be able to tackle the above types of crimes, what steps would you suggest to effectively deal with these types of crimes? (We have in mind the case of left wing)

(47) What organizational structure has the State got or proposes to set up to handle organized crime? Are you envisaging any special legislation to handle organized crimes?

(48) Has your State got any special legislation to control terrorism or organized crime? Are you contemplating any such legislation?

Recruitment

(49) Entry age into the IPS used to be 20 to 24 years. However some years ago it has been raised to 21 to 27 years. There is a feeling that late entry into the service affects the trainability and moulding the character of the ranks right

lines for good policing. While this is also true of other All India Services, in the case of police service the matter acquires greater seriousness. What are your views on reducing the age of entry for the IPS officers back to 20-24.

(50) The same is true regarding recruitment to other ranks of the police force. What are your views?

(51) Do you think that a special legislation is necessary to deal with certain offences by police personnel like surrending the weapons, cowardice, deserting the police station under threat etc. to avoid the cumbersome and time consuming departmental enquiries.

Recruitment of Constables

(52) What is the minimum qualification for recruitment of Constables to various Wings of Police: Civil, Armed, others?

(53) Do you think that the minimum qualification should be a Graduate Degree, since the police would increasingly be called upon to handle sophisticated crime and criminals, and for a better quality of public-police interface?

(54) Since a very large number of mediocre candidates appear for the post of constables, should there be a pre-qualifying examination, based on General Knowledge, Comprehension, etc. and/or, Attitudinal aspects?

(55) What is the composition of the Recruitment Boards? Are they entirely departmental, or, are there outside persons?

(56) Do you think that the recruitment of constables should be done at a zonal or State level, instead of at the district level as at present. Should the constable cadre be a zonal cadre instead of a district cadre?

(57) How to make the entire selection process, including examination, interview, physical fitness and medical tests transparent and free from corrupt practices?

(58) Are the annual requirements of constabulary assessed regularly, and recruitments made every year? When did the last two recruitments take place?

Recruitment of Sub-Inspectors

(59) If you agree that the minimum qualification for recruitment of a civil constable should be 'graduation', do you think that there should be direct recruitment of Sub-Inspectors?

(60) Is the recruitment made by State Public Service Commission or, Staff Selection Committees, with at least some outsiders, or, is it done purely departmentally?

(61) What is the weightage of marks given for Written Test and for Interviews?

(62) What is the percentage of Sub-Inspectors' Posts filled by direct recruitment and by departmental promotion?

(63) What steps are needed to ensure physical fitness and alertness in police personnel of all ranks?

(64) What are the levels at which direct entry should be made in police?

(65) What kind of attitude and behavior do you expect from a policeman? Please list four of them in order of priority. How can we ensure proper selection of the right personnel with the right attitude in police? What reforms need to be made in the present recruitment procedure?

(66) What percentage of posts at the direct entry levels should be filled by fresh recruitment?

Training

(67) Do you think the present system of training is suitable for a community friendly, service oriented law enforcement agency? If not what is wrong?

(68) Do you think the present system of out-door training serves a useful purpose? Do you think there is scope for modification in the present outdoor training? Explain.

(69) Apart from the initial training of new entrants, there should be a continuous process of training spanning over the whole career of all police personnel. Are you satisfied with the present in-service training? If not what suggestions do you have ?

(70) How can training be made more practical, effective and popular?

Police Station

(71) Do you think the present police stations are well equipped to tackle the problems of the near future? What changes would you envisage?

(72) Do you think the present police set-up at the station level inspires confidence in the public, especially the socially disadvantaged sections? What suggestions do you have to improve the situation?

(73) What steps are necessary to improve the working at police station level to meet the emerging requirements of crime prevention, detection, Law and Order, and people's expectations, particularly, the socially disadvantaged sections in terms of:

1. Appearance of the Police Station
2. Facilities for public, who approach the Station
3. Rank of the Station House Officer
4. Composition and number of policemen/staff at the station
5. Vehicles, drivers, petrol/diesel
6. Supply of stationery, forms

7. Phones/computers/typewriters/wireless
8. Weapons
9. Funds for upkeep of the police station, and equipment
10. Aids to investigation
11. Any other

Computerization

(74) It is admitted by all that computerization of police working would improve their efficiency manifold. The basic requisites for nation-wide computerization of criminal records are : (a) commitment for computerization amongst the higher echelons of police hierarchy, (b) high priority, with requisite findings, by political leadership, (c) developing an All-India perspective, which, in turn, calls for standardization of forms, right from police station level for recording and reporting crime. What steps are being taken to enforce these basic requirements?

(75) There is a view that, at the time of direct recruitment to various ranks, and for promotions within the Department, a weightage should be given to those who have a diploma/ certificate in computer skills?

What are your views?

Human Rights

(76) It is said that 60 per cent of the arrests made by police in the Country, are really unnecessary. This is in addition to the totally unauthorized detentions in the police station which are not even recorded. An unnecessary arrest becomes the starting point for further human rights violations, like beating up in lock up, etc.

What steps do you think need to be taken to eliminate unnecessary arrests?

(77) Another major reason for people feeling harassed by the police is the non-registration of crime when people approach the police stations.

What suggestions you have to see that the malady is rectified?

Work-load and Morale

(78) One of the arguments advanced is that police have no clearly designed work-hours, that they on occasions spend days together in the police stations, and that the resulting stress and loss of morale, tells on their behaviour with the people who approach them. It is argued that an 8-hour shift system should be introduced in policing, like in many countries around the world. What are your views?

(79) What steps do you suggest to bring about a change in the attitudes, mindset, and behaviour of individual policeman, the group behaviour of the police, and the beahaviour of police as a Force?

(80) One of the constant criticisms is that the Government of the day uses the police for enhancing its political clout. The Government uses the power of transfers and postings to exercise its influence to further its ends.

What are your views for providing a reasonable tenure to the three important levels in police, namely, the SHOs, the SPs and the DGs of police? What machinery would you suggest to see that the transfers made are in public interest and not in political interest? What mechanisms are necessary to ensure that the police perform their legitimate duties without the fear of uncalled for interference from outside, at the same time, ensuring the accountability of the police for their acts of commission and omission?

(81) In the above context there is a suggestion that the DG of Police should be from outside, i.e, from a different cadre, What are your views?

(82) Do you think that any legislative changes are required in the Police Act of your State in the above connection?

(83) What is your assessment in a scale of 0-10 about the role of police leadership and their performance in seeing that the Police Force they command, also commands the goodwill and respect of the public?

(84) Political interference in police working is being depicted as a major handicap in the efficient functioning of police. Do you feel this is correct? How prevalent is it in your State?

(85) How do we insulate police at various levels from undue political interference without taking away its accountability?

(86) Do you think that any amendments are called for in the Police Acts, IPC/Cr. P.C/Evidence Act to have more effective policing in all its aspects?

Bibliography

Acharya, B.K., *Codification in British India*, Tagore Law Lectures (1912), S.K. Banerji & Sons, Calcutta, 1914

Arnold Devid , *Police Power and Colonial Rule*, Madras (1859-1947), Oxford University Press, Madras, 1986

Auber, Peter, *Rise and Progress of the British Power in India*, Vol. I & II, W.M.H. Allen & Co., and Calkim & Pall Mal, 1837

Bani Prasad, *State in Ancient India,* The Indian Press, Allahabad, 1926

Bayley, David, *H., The Police and Political Development in India*, Princeton, New Jersey, 1969

Berkley, G.E., *The Democratic Policemen,* Beacon Press, Beston, 1969

Besant, Annie, *How India Wrought for Freedom*, Theosophical Publishing House, Adyar, Madras, 1915

Bhardwaj, R.K., *Indian Police Administration*, National, New Delhi, 1978

Bikshit, R.C., *Independent India and Its Keepers of Peace*, CBI Bulletin, Vol. V, No.10, Oct.1997

Buxi, U., *The Crisis of the Indian Legal System*, Vikas, New Delhi, 1982

Chatterji, S.K., *The Police in Ancient India*, The Indian Police Journal (1861 - 1961), Indian Police Centenary Edition, 1961

Chhabra, G.S., *Advanced Study in the History of Modern India*, Sharanjit, Jullunder City, 1908

Coloso, F.T.R. and Shukla, K.S., *Reluctance of the Public to Aid the Police in the Detection of Crime and Crime Reporting at Police_Stations*, B.P.R & D., Govt., of India, Delhi, 1973

Curry, J.C., *The Indian Police*, Manu Publications, New Delhi, 1977

Erayil, A.L. and James Vadackumchery, *Police and the Society*, Kairali Books International, Trivandrum, 1985

Fawelt, C., *The First Century of British Justice in India*, Clarendon Press, Oxford, 1934

Felkeness, G.T., *Attitudes Police Officers Towards Their Professional Ethics*, Journal of Criminal Justice, 12 (3), 211 -220, 1984

German, A.C., *Police Personnel Management*, Charles C. Thomas, Springfield, 1958

Ghosh, S.K. and K.F. Rustamji, *Encyclopaedia of Police in India* (Vol. I), Ashish Publishing House, Delhi, 1993

Gopal, S., *British Policy in India: 1858 - 1905*, Cambridge University Press, Cambridge, 1965

Gouldsbury, C.E., *Life in the Indian Police*, Chapman & Hall, London, 1912

Gourley, N.R., *A Contribution Towards a History of Police in Bengal*, Secretariat Press, Bengal, 1916

Griffiths, P.J., *The British Impact on India*, Mac donald, London, 1952

Hariharan, A., *Humanising the Police*, Hindustan Times, Dec. 26, 1980

Hollins, S.T., No Ten Commandments, *Life in the Indian Police*, Hutchinson, London, 1954

Hooja, M.M.L., *Police During the British Rule*, The Indian Police Journal (1861 - 1961), Centenary Issue, 1961

Jain, M.P., *Outlines of Indian Legal History*, University Press, Delhi

Jonkins, Robert, *Keeping the Police,* Harper and Row, New York, 1970

Kamte, N.M. and Telang, V.K., *The Police in India and Abroad*, M.T. Kamte House, Pune, 1980

Karve, D.G. Police Administration in India: *A Re-appraisal of the Aims and Means*, Indian Journal of Public Administration, Oct - Dec., 1956, 307-15

Kripalani, J.B., *Our Police During Emergency*, Indian Express, 31 May, 1977

Kulshrestha, V.D., *Landmarks in the Indian Legal History*, Eastern Book Agency, Lucknow & Delhi, 1959

Madan, J.C., *Indian Police: Its Development up to 1905: An Historical Analysis*, Uppal Publishing House, Delhi, 1980

Mann, T.K., *Administration of Justice in India*, Concept, New Delhi, 1979

Misra, B.B., *The Administrative History of India*: 1834 - 1947, Oxford University Press, New Delhi, 1970

Moore, R.J., *Liberalism and Indian Politics*: 1872-1922, Edward Arnold, London, 1966

Morley, W.H., *Administration of Justice in British India*, Metropolitan, New Delhi, 1976

Mosse, George L. (ed.), *Police Forces in History*, Sage Publications, Baverly Hills (CA), 1975

Mullick, B.N., *A Philosophy for the Police*, Allied Publishers, New Delhi, 1969

Nath, Trilok, The Indian Police: *A Case for a New Image*, Sterling Publishers Pvt. Ltd., New Delhi, 1978

Pandey A.K., *Policing in Ancient India*, The Indian Police Journal, Vol. XXXII, No. 2., April - June, 1985

Parliamentary Papers (Published), *House of Commons Papers*, 1855-1905

Proceedings of the Home Department (Manuscript Sources: unpublished), *Police Branch*, 1862 - 1906

Pylee, M.V., *Constitutional Government in India*, Asia Publishing House, Bombay, 1960

Rao, K.V., *Parliamentary Democracy of India*, The World Press (P) Ltd., Calcutta, 1961

Rao, S.V., *Police Under the East India Company*, The Indian Police Journal (1861-1961), Centenary Issue, 1961

Reith, Charles, *British Police and the Democratic Ideal*, Oxford University Press, London, 1943

Report of the Beames' Committee of Bengal, 1891

Report of the Commission for the Investigation of alleged cases of Torture at Madras - 1855

Report of the Indian Police Commission: 1902-03

Report of the Kerala Reorganization Committee, 1959

Reports of the National Police Commission: 1977-81

Report of the Police Committee, 1838

Report of the Police Commission, 1860

Ruchelman, L (ed.), *Who Rules the Police*, New York University Press, New York, 1973

Saha, B.P., *Indian Police Legacy and Quest For Formative Role*, Konark Publishers Ltd., Delhi, 1990

Sarkar, J.N., *Police System in Medieval India in Theory and Practice*, The Indian Police Journal, 1861-1961, Centenary Issue, 1961

Sengupta, S.S., *Work Culture in Police Administration*, Ashish Publishing House, New Delhi, 1995

Sharma, P.D., *Police, Polity and People in India*, Uppal Publishing House, New Delhi, 1981

Singh, Hira Lal, *Problems and Politics of the British in India*: 1885-1898, Asia Publishing House, London, 1963

Sinha, B.P., *Indian Police Legacy and Quest for Formative Role*, Konark Publishers Pvt. Ltd., Delhi, 1990

Sinha, S.K., *The Police in India*, USI Journal, April-June, 1970

Spangenberg, *Bradford, British Bureaucracy in India: Status, Policy and the I.C.S., in the Late 19th Century*, Manohar, Delhi, 1976

Stokes, Erick, *The English Utilitarians and India*, The Clarendon Press, Oxford, 1959

The Calcutta Gazette, 13 October, 1960

The Gazette of India, 16 February, 1872

The Indian Police Act (Act V) of 1861

Thomson, Craig, *The Police State*, Dutton, New York, 1950

Vadackumchery, James, *Indian Police and Miscarriage of Justice*, A.P.H. Publishing Corporation, New Delhi, 1997

Vadackumchery James, *Management Thoughts on Police Administration*, A.P.H. Publishing Corporation, New Delhi, 1997

Webster, John, A., *The Realities of Police Work*, Kendall Hunt, Babugue, 1973

Westley, W.A., *Violence and the Police*, American Journal of Sociology, 59, 34, 1953

Younger, E.J., *Challenges to Police in Changing World*, Indian Police Journal (Jan-March), 1970

Index

❑❑❑